How To Live A Debt Free Life

Get Out Of Debt And Stay Out Of Debt.

By
Peter Wilmore

Pratzen Publishing

Copyright Notice

Copyright © Pratzen Publishing 2007. All rights reserved. None of the materials in this publication may be used, reproduced or transmitted, in whole or in part, in any form or by any means, electronic or mechanical, including photocopying, recording or the use of any information storage and retrieval system, without permission in writing from the publisher. To request such permission and for further inquiries, contact:

Pratzen Publishing, 512 NE 81st Street, Ste. F #171 , Vancouver, WA 98665

First Edition: 2007

ISBN 978-1461061991

Trademark Disclaimer

Product names, logos, brands, URLs, web site links, and other trademarks featured or referred to within this publication or within any supplemental or related materials are the property of their respective trademark holders. These trademark holders are not affiliated with the author or publisher and the trademark holders do not sponsor or endorse our materials.

Copyright Acknowledgement

Photographs attributed to a third party are the property of such third party and are used here by permission. All such attributed photographs are subject to the copyright claims of each respective owner.

Legal Disclaimer

This publication provides information about financial matters and includes references to certain legal and accounting principles. Although the author and the publisher believe that the included information is accurate and useful, nothing contained in this publication can be considered professional advice on any legal or accounting matter. You must consult a licensed attorney or accountant if you want professional advice that is appropriate to your particular situation.

"God Helps Those Who Help Themselves"

Motto of the Confederate Raider C.S.S. Alabama

Table Of Contents

Preface…………………………………………………………	7
Assessing Your Situation……………………………………..	11
Budgeting & Setting Goals……………………………………	31
Cost Cutting & Increasing Your Income……………………	43
Eliminate Your Debt…………………………………………	61
Banks & Bank Accounts…………………………………….	77
Saving Your Money………………………………………….	89
Investing Your Money ……………………………………..	101
Insurance: Protecting What You Have……………………..	119
Taxes…………………………………………………………	129
Afterword……………………………………………………	141

Preface

When I first went to college right out of high school I filled out several applications for so called "Student Credit Cards". At the time, I had no need for credit cards. My parents paid for my tuition and books and I had a part time job that supplied me with my spending money. At the time, I thought that if I had and used several credit cards responsibly, I would build my credit in the future. Armed with a long history of responsible credit use, I could then qualify for mortgages and auto loans with lower rates and save myself a great deal of money in interest. It was going to be perfect.

That was the plan. Unfortunately, that is not how things worked out. Before I knew it, I had in my wallet, four credit cards with a total limit of $2500. To many people that may seem like a paltry sum. However, I was young, and I did not fully appreciate the danger that I was courting. My income at the time was small. I earned on average $250 a week working in the restaurant industry. I also had a steady girlfriend for the first time in my life as well.

Sooner than I knew what was happening, I had maxed out each of the cards. I had gone out and used them for everything. I had bought books and clothes that I wanted. I had paid for dates with my girlfriend that I could not really afford. Let me tell you, if you have to finance your dinner out, you are probably best doing without it. However, again, I was young and stupid. I kept up with the minimum payments for a while and my credit did improve as I had planned.

I used my new found credit worthiness to qualify for an auto loan. I signed up for cell phones (yes, plural) and other luxuries I did not need, but I thought enhanced my status and completed me as a person. I even added credit cards to my wallet, and charged those cards to the limit as well. I still kept up with the minimum payments and everything was fine, even though I did not know I was starting to drown in debt.

Interest that was accruing never occurred to me. It did not matter that I was in debt to the total of my income for a year. I had no savings and I was living paycheck to paycheck. This did not matter either.

I never told my parents what was happening. I did not even think that I was in trouble. Why would I mention it to them? I did not tell my girlfriend either. No one knew that I was in trouble and I refused to admit the possibility either.

One thing led to another. I changed jobs and my income dipped for a little while. I forgot to send in some payments and late charges were applied. Things quickly multiplied from there and spiraled out of control. Cards were canceled by the banks that issued them for nonpayment. I stopped paying a lot of my bills for one reason or another. Tuition was not paid. Instead of writing the checks with the money my parents gave me, I spent it on all sorts of ill-conceived notions. Creditors began to call me everyday. Checks that I wrote bounced. My bank accounts were finally closed while still overdrawn. People came to repossess my car. Insurance premiums were not paid. Most of the bills were in collection and I generally contented myself to paying only my monthly bills like rent and utilities, although, even these were not always paid and almost never on time.

Things were a mess and I was so overwhelmed by the sheer magnitude of the debts that I just stopped caring, at least outwardly. Inside I was also a mess. I lost sleep and worried all the time about these debts. I feared going to the mail box because I knew inside were colored envelopes (bill collectors almost always use colored envelopes to get your attention). I never answered the phone unless I knew who it was. I was afraid to look the problem in the eye and I was absolutely not going to take responsibility for creating this mess.

On the day of my 23 birthday I hit rock bottom. I was driving home late in my beat up worn out car when it lost power. I managed to pull into a local grocery store parking lot and I tried to figure out what was wrong. I could do nothing to get it working. I was about to panic. Without my car I could not get to work and I had $0 to my name. I did not even have a bank account at the time. My wife (then she was my girlfriend and had no idea of my financial problems) was kind enough to let me use her AAA card to get the car towed to a repair shop. The shop was closed and I left a message for them describing the problem. It turned out the timing belt had broken and was going to cost $450 dollars to be repaired. I did not have the money and I had no idea how I was going to pay for the repair. That is when I made the call that every young person should dread. I called my parents to explain to them why I needed them to send me money to bail me out of trouble.

My parents are good people and I love them very much. However, when I hung up the phone I felt as low as I ever have in my life. Here I was 23 and living on my own, calling home to mommy and daddy crying for help. They agreed to pay for the repair. They did also give me a priceless birthday gift that night. They gave me the sting of feeling absolutely pathetic that motivated me to take responsibility for my situation and to fix it. The repair was helpful, but the sting is what I will ever be thankful for.

To make a long story short, I finally looked my problems in the eye and I began to fix them. One by one, I eliminated debts and built my savings. Once I was debt free, I began to build my personal wealth, and as I did so, I fixed my credit.

What follows in the rest of this book are the philosophies and the methods that made me debt free and financially independent. No I am not a rich man. I still work and I wrote this book in my spare time. However, I have saved a pretty penny. I own my home and I have good credit. I have enough to see me through emergencies and to take a nice vacation each year. I live a good life and I have not worried about a bill collector for years.

You may be just like I was. You may not sleep at night. You may dread the mailbox and you may think that your problems are too overwhelming for you to beat. You might just want to save a little money and start planning for retirement. This book might help you. Everything in this book is the product of my personal experience and there is a light at the end of the tunnel, even if you cannot see it. Hopefully when you are finished with this book, you will be armed with the knowledge to get started. It was not easy. You will have to make sacrifices at times and you will need to make hard decisions. You will have to take responsibility and you will need to focus. The quote on the dedication page is there for a reason. Read it over and no matter what your religion or thoughts on God, realize that only you can dig out of this hole. If you believe that, I have high hopes that you can succeed and I wish you the best of luck.

-Peter Wilmore

Chapter 1
Assessing Your Situation

If you have purchased this book, chances are you feel that there is some problem with the health of your finances. Maybe you are swimming in debt. Maybe you have no savings or bank account. Maybe you have nothing saved for retirement. This book can help with all of these problems.

No problem can be solved without first identifying it. Your particular situation is no exception to this rule. In this chapter we are going to discuss how to look your problem in the eye. In following chapters we will begin to plan how to overcome it.

It is not an understatement to say that this is by far the most important chapter in this book. The ideas shared in this chapter and the information you gather and organize should be in the back of your mind the rest of this book. You should also repeat this process each month. Without correct and up to date information, an accurate picture of your financial situation cannot be created. Without this picture you will not have any idea where you stand, what needs to be improved and where you are doing well.

One last topic I wish to discuss, prior to diving into this chapter, is honesty. This can be tough. During this chapter you will be asking yourself a lot of questions and providing the answers to these. Some of these questions may not have answers that you like and some of them may be very uncomfortable to think about. This is the first of the hurdles that you must overcome on your path to financial responsibility and freedom. You must provide honest and truthful answers no matter how hard they are. Without honest answers you cannot begin to help yourself.

Definition of "Financial Independence"

This book will make many references to "Financial Independence". I want to make sure that this term is well defined and we agree on its meaning right from the beginning. For the purposes of this book, "Financial Independence" means that you are not dependent on any other person, live debt free (except for maybe a mortgage) and you are able to support yourself in a comfortable lifestyle. Any references to "Financial Independence" in this book will reference this definition.

"Financial Independence" does not mean that you are worth a billion dollars and can buy and sell people. It does not mean that you are the star of your own reality show or anything like that. As stated in the paragraph above, it simply means that you have enough financial resources to live comfortably and that you do not live "paycheck to paycheck".

1.1 Your Financial Awareness

You may have bought this book for any number of reasons. You may have liked the title or cover art. You may have received it as a gift. However, the chances are good, that if you bought this book you may feel you have a problem with your finances and the idea of financial independence appeals to you. You may be in debt or you may want to learn how to start saving and investing for retirement. Any way you slice it you are going to need to begin by finding the areas in your financial life that need improvement and establishing realistic goals to improve them.

In order to find areas of your financial life that need improvement you should complete Worksheet 1.1. This is a simple Q and A form that will give you some very good insight into your particular financial situation and where you need to devote your energies. If you do not know the answers to any of these questions, proudly write down "I Do Not Know". This is not bad at all. The smartest thing anyone can do is say "I Do Not Know". Only then are you being honest with yourself and can create a situation where you can learn the answer.

Specific inquiries into your situation such as obtaining your credit files and histories and recording your expenses will be accomplished later. Worksheet 1 is a way to examine your perceptions and general knowledge about your financial situation before we start.

Worksheet 1.1:Before Getting Started

A. Money Management

   1. How much do you spend in an average week?
   2. Do you prefer to pay cash or do you use cards?
   3. What luxuries do you buy each day/week? Include newspapers, lattes, movies etc.
   4. What do spend your money on?
   5. Do you have a budget? How is this determined?
   6. How often do you use an ATM?
   7. Are you concerned by your spending?

B. Debt
   1. How much money do you owe?
   2. To whom do you owe this money?
   3. What do you owe money for? Are you paying for cars, appliances, a house, education, etc.?
   4. How much money do you pay in interest each month?
   5. What are the interest rates on every loan or credit card that you have? List each one.
   6. Are any bills past due?
   7. Do you ever pay late fees or overdraft fees? How often?
   8. Are any of your bills more that 90 days late or in collections?
   9. Do you receive letters from collection agencies or creditors? When was the last time this happened?
   10. Do you receive phone calls at work or home from creditors? When was the last time this happened?
   11. Do you worry about your debts? Do you lose sleep?

C. Expenses
   1. How much are your total expenses each month?
   2. How much do you spend on food, gas, housing, and utilities?
   3. How much do you spend on nonessential services such as cable, internet, gym memberships, movies etc.?
   4. Do your expenses vary with time? For example, do you spend more for electricity in the winter?
   5. If you lost your primary source of income, how much would you need to live the way you do for three months?
   6. Do you have a car? How much do you pay for it each month? How much does your insurance cost? How much does gas cost?

7. If you use public transportation, how much does it cost?
8. Do you wish to lower your expenses?

D. Savings
   1. How much do you have saved up?
   2. How much do you save each month?
   3. Where do you keep your savings?
   4. When was the last time you dipped into your savings?
   5. Why did you dip into your savings?
   6. How long would your savings support your lifestyle if you had no income?
   7. How much do you have saved in special retirement accounts? An example of this is a work 401(k).
   8. How much do you believe you need to save for retirement?
   9. Do you believe you are saving enough?

E. Banking
   1. Do you have a bank account? If not, can you open one if you wanted to?
   2. Are your accounts in good standing with positive balances?
   3. What type of bank account(s) do you have?
   4. How much do you have in each one of your accounts?
   5. What interest is paid on these accounts?
   6. What monthly fees do your accounts have?
   7. Have you had any overdrafts or bounced checks lately?

F. Income
   1. In the previous tax year, what was your income on your "W-2s"?
   2. How much do you earn per week?
   3. Are you salaried or are you paid by the hour?
   4. When was the last time you received a raise?

5. Are you happy with your current job?

G. Investment

1. Do you know what a stock, bond, mutual fund or REIT is?
2. Have you ever invested before?
3. How much have you or do you have invested?
4. What are you invested in?
5. What do these companies do? What types of bonds do you hold?
6. What was the last financial or business news article you read?
7. Do you know how to buy stocks or bonds?
8. Do you have a 401(k), IRA or Roth IRA?
9. Do you feel that you are investing enough?

Once you have answered all of these questions to the best of your ability, you should sit down and look over your answers. These can tell you a lot about both your knowledge of your finances and the health of those finances.

1.2 Collecting Your Information

Bills, Receipts and Statements ... Oh My!

Now that you have worked your way through Worksheet 1, you need to collect and organize a good deal of information and actually construct an honest accurate picture of your finances.

To accomplish this goal will take 30 days. This may seem like a long time but, we need to remember that Rome was not built in a day, and your financial freedom will take some time as well. You will need to start with a box of some kind. This box is where you will put each and every financial document that you receive over the course of the next 30 days. This includes receipts of any kind, bills, bank statements, collection letters, credit card statements, tax notices, insurance statements, investment statements, etc. You will, of course, pay every bill on time. However, the part that is left for your records will go into the box.

Credit Reports

While you are waiting for 30 days to acquire all of your financial documents, you can busy yourself with obtaining your credit files.

In America today, there are three leading credit bureaus. These are, in no particular order, Experian (http://www.experian.com), TransUnion (http://www.transunion.com) , and Equifax (http://www.equifax.com) . Whenever you apply for credit cards, auto loans or mortgages in this country, the lender will examine your credit file, with at least one and possibly all three of these companies. This means that you have a strong interest in making sure all of the information in these files is true and accurate.

Your credit file is also a great way to find out if you owe anyone money. If you do owe money, say from a bill you forgot when you were 21, or from someone you thought you paid, your credit file will show this. Along with the debt, the contact information of the debt holder will be listed.

In my personal situation my credit file was an essential tool in eliminating my debt. I was able to see on several pages, there were a total of about 19 negative records listed, who I owed money to and how much I owed them. Several of the collection agencies had never contacted me via mail and I was completely unaware of the debts. Without looking at my credit file, I never would have known about these and the debts which would have continued accruing interest and haunting my credit history for a long time.

Obtaining your credit file is not a terribly complicated process but it may take a little time. You can contact each of the above listed credit bureaus through their websites and purchase a copy of your credit file. The fees are not terrible and the information will be provided immediately online. Be prepared to provide your birth date and Social Security Number (SSN). You will also have to answer questions about your credit file such as how much your monthly car payment is and from which bank you got the loan so be prepared for that. This is and added security feature to help prevent identity theft.

If you have been turned down for credit of any kind within the last 60 days, you can request free of charge, a copy of your credit report from the credit bureaus. Write each bureau a letter stating that you have been denied credit within the 60 day window. A sample letter to do this is shown in Example 1.2. You will need to list you name, address, SSN, birth date and phone number. This is thanks to a law known as the Fair Credit Reporting Act (FCRA). The fair credit reporting act can also be used to remove incorrect information from your credit file. To see the full text of the law visit http://www.ftc.gov/os/statutes/031224fcra.pdf.

Date

Dear Credit Reporting Agency;

I have been denied credit within the last 60 days based on information provided by your firm. According to the Fair Credit Reporting Act, I am entitled to receive a <u>FREE</u> copy of my credit report. This letter is a formal request for a free copy of my report.

My information is as follows:
My name is John Sample
My address is 123 Any Street, Anytown, USA
My social security number is 555-55-5555
My birth date is XX/XX/XXXX

Thank you;
Sign Your Name
<u>**Example 1.2**</u> **Sample Credit Report Request Letter**

The last method of obtaining your credit report is to sign up for a credit monitoring service. These are easily found on the internet. These services will provide you with access to your credit file, credit score, and will alert you each time a new inquiry is made into your credit file or when a new account is opened. There is a monthly fee for these services which should cost you no more than $10 a month. If the service you are looking at cost more than that, keep looking. Also make sure that the service you sign up for will provide you with an updated report and score from ALL three credit bureaus (known as a "triple bureau report") every 30 days. An outdated report is of little value. This method of getting your credit report is my personal favorite. It allows you, at a set low fee, to have constant, intimate, access to this information whenever you need it.

Print out a copy of triple bureau report and put it in your box. We will need that information as well for our detailed analysis.

Chexsytems

In addition to the three credit bureaus, banks report delinquent accounts to a company called Chexsystems (http://www.consumerdebit.com) . If your bank accounts have been closed by a bank for mishandling, you will have a file with this company. I myself was listed with this company and it made opening a bank account very difficult. Banks did not want me as a customer because of my poor history.

Chexsystems is governed by the FCRA as well. If you have been denied a bank account because of information provided by Chexsystems you can request, again free of charge, a copy of your file through their website. If you are listed in Chexsystems, you will need to obtain a copy of this report and place it in your box. This information, again, will be very helpful to our analysis.

1.3   Analyzing Your Records

Now that you have all of your credit files, and you have all of your financial documents from the last 30 days, we can begin to analyze your financial status. It is a good idea to have a notebook to record all of this information and to keep things tidy.

We firstly need to sort the financial documents into useful categories. From there we can understand particular aspects of your financial picture. Sort your documents and receipts into:

1. Receipts for items purchased with cash
2. Receipts for items purchased with a credit/debit card
3. Bank statements
4. Brokerage statements
5. Credit card bills
6. Utility bills

7. Pay stubs and tax returns
8. Insurance bills
9. Credit reports
10. Collection letters, late bills and overdraft notices

It's OK if you do not have documents for a particular category. However, most of your documents should fit into one of the above.

Once you have all of your papers in nice organized piles we can begin to examine and extract information from each one. Let's examine each one in its turn.

Receipts From Cash Purchases

This pile of papers will tell you how much you purchase with cash in 30 days. Total up all of the receipts. Next answer these questions:

1. How much cash did you spend last month?
2. How much of this spending was for necessary items? Examples of necessary items are food from a supermarket, gas, rent, or utilities.
3. How much of this cash spending was for luxury or unnecessary items? Examples of luxury items are food from restaurants, lattes on the way to work, magazines, or movies.
4. Is this amount of cash spending more or less than what you expected?
5. Do you think this amount of spending is acceptable? What can you do to reduce your cash spending?

Cash can be a very dangerous thing to carry in your pocket. Many people do not concern themselves with spending cash and are quick to do so. Many times they are convinced to buy things they do not need because they have cash to pay for it. Many people (I am one of these people) prefer to limit their spending with a cash allowance. When the cash is gone, they are done spending money. Which one sounds like you?

Receipts From Credit/Debit Card Purchases

The next pile of paperwork that you need to go through is your pile of receipts from card transactions. This pile, like the proceeding pile, will give you a better idea of your spending habits with a particular for of payment- namely plastic. This can be a problem area for a lot of people. I was no exception to this. Many people simply pull out their cards and use them whenever they need something. Little thought is given to the bill that will be received at the end of the month, the debt that is being created or the account whose balance is being drawn down.

Ask yourself the same questions as you did for cash, only with regard to your plastic spending. What do the answers tell you? Is your spending what you thought it was?

Bank Statements

Looking at your receipts will give you a good understanding of your spending habits. Looking over your bank statements will inform you about your relationship with any banks that you do business with. Examining these documents will also give you a good idea of your available savings cushion. Ask yourself these questions:

1. What was your average balance during the last 30 days?
2. Do you consider this amount to be a healthy cushion to protect you from unforeseen expenses?
3. Was your balance always positive?
4. If it was not always positive, how many days was your account overdrawn?
5. If your account was ever overdrawn, what caused this? Was it a fee, a check, a withdrawal or a card purchase?
6. Did you pay any overdraft fees? How much were these?
7. Did you pay any fees for your account? Examples of these are fees for balances below an established minimum or excessive transaction fees.

Brokerage Statements

Many people suffer from investing ignorance. They take little interest in investing and could not care less about where their money is invested. Maybe their parents or spouse established their accounts or perhaps they signed up with a 401(k) program at work. Whatever the reason, if this is a condition that you suffer from, you must overcome it. To be financially independent and responsible, you will need to know where your money is invested, how much is invested and how these investments have been performing over time. Your brokerage statements will be of immense value in this regard. Carefully study these documents and answer these questions:

1. What is the total value of all my investments?
2. What types of investments do I have? Are they stocks, bonds or a combination of stocks and bonds? Real estate?
3. What income have I received from these investments?
4. Brokerage statements commonly show a beginning of the month balance and an end of the month balance. What are these? Have your investments gained value or lost value this month?
5. In addition to monthly balances, brokerage statements commonly show year to date balances. Over the course of the current year how have you investments performed? Have they gained or lost value?

In a later chapter we will explore just what types of investments you have and what they mean. However, for now just get a general feeling of how they are doing and whether they are stocks, bonds, a combination, real estate, etc.

Credit Card Bills

We already examined the ways that you use your credit cards to pay for goods and services. The precious information on your credit card statements that would be difficult to find in other places is how much this is costing you. Look over your bills and discover **for each card you have**:

1. How much of a balance are you carrying?
2. How much did you pay in finances charges last month?
3. Did you pay any late fees?
4. How much is your cards annual fee?
5. What is your credit limit?
6. What is the percentage of credit that you are using? For example, a balance of $50 and a limit of $500 means you are using 10% of your credit.

In addition to asking yourself these questions and finding the answers, you should also find out the interest rate on each and every credit card. These rates will generally fall somewhere between 10%-20% annually.

Utility Bills

Utility bills normally include gas, water, electric, garbage, and sewer usage. However, today you can include telephone, cable and internet with utilities as well. These statements will tell you how much of these services your household is consuming. It is a great idea to track these expenses and this information will be valuable when you begin to construct a budget. You can also begin to think about shaving some of these costs down. Ask yourself:

1. How can I lower my electricity bills? Is it cheaper to have a fan or air conditioning?
2. Can I lower my garbage bill by recycling more?
3. Do I really need all of those premium cable channels? Do I really need or can I really afford cable?
4. How much is my internet costing me? Do I need that fast of a connection and is there a less expensive option?
5. Can I bundle the services I am receiving with one company for a cheaper package deal?

Pay stubs, Taxes

Your pay stubs will contain a wealth of information about your income. Firstly, your rate of pay if you are hourly or your monthly salary will be listed. Your income will be listed as the pay you receive on the current check and you will frequently find a year to date figure as well. You will be surprised to find out how many people do no know how much they earn. They may have a fairly good idea but cannot name the amount to the penny. With finances, you will find the devil is in the detail and you should know this information by heart.

In addition to your pay, you will find other useful information. You will find out how much is being withheld for federal (usually listed as FICA) and state taxes as well as Medicare and Social Security taxes. This information, as well, will be listed for the current pay period and year to date. You will see you how many exemptions you are currently claiming. This number determines how much money is withheld from your pay for taxes.

Lastly you will be able to find any pension, 401(k), insurance withholdings or garnishments (when debt collectors forcibly take money from your check due to a court judgement). These will be listed near your tax information and should also be listed by current pay period and year to date. If your employer matches any contributions to your 401(k), this will be listed too.

Answer all of the following questions:

1. What is your hourly rate of pay or how much are you paid each month if you are a salaried employee?
2. How much was your pre-tax income for the past month? How much did you actually take home? How much have you earned for the current year?
3. How much did you pay in federal, state, Medicare, and Social Security taxes this pay period? How much have you paid during the current year?
4. How many exemptions are you currently claiming?
5. Do you have any insurance, pension or 401(k) withholdings? How much was withheld this month and year to date?
6. If you have a 401(k), is there a match? If there is a match, how much did you receive this month and year?

Insurance Bills

Most people obtain their medical insurance through their employers. However, some people do not. In addition, most people carry private auto, disability and life insurance. In your quest for financial responsibility, you will need to understand not only what you pay, but what type of coverage you are carrying. Answer the following questions:

1. What is the monthly premium for each policy I carry?
2. Who provides these policies? Are these policies through one company or several?
3. For life insurance is it whole life or term life? How much coverage do you have?
4. For auto insurance, determine if you carry comprehensive or liability only. What is you maximum coverage per accident? Are there any medical provisions to this policy?

5. If you carry disability insurance how much would you be paid each month? Is this enough to pay all of your bills?
6. Most disability policies require you to be out of work for a certain period before receiving benefits. How long is this period for your policy?

Credit Reports

Now you will need to look at your credit reports. You should have in your possession three reports, one from each of the three credit bureaus. Study these documents very carefully. Inside these pages you will find many excellent indicators of your current financial situation as well as your strengths and weaknesses. Perhaps you have too many credit cards or perhaps you have paid every bill on time your entire life. You should also have a total of three credit scores as well. When studying these documents a few things to ask would be:

1. What are your three credit scores?
2. What is your average credit score? You can determine this number by adding all three together and dividing by three.
3. What is the oldest account in your credit file? Each record should list the date on which it was created. This establishes the length of your credit history.
4. What is your credit history? Have you missed payments? Have you always paid on time?
5. Are there any records from collection agencies? Are there any records listed as "charge off"?
6. Are all of the records correct? Do you recognize and remember each of the records listed?
7. How many active accounts does each file list?
8. Each file should list your total debt and your total credit. What is you total listed debt on each record? What is your total listed credit?
9. Is all of your personal information correct? Examples of personal information include your current address, past addresses, and employers.

Collection Letters and Late Bills

You may not have any documents that fit into this category. If you do not have any of these, I congratulate you. Perhaps you are like I was and have enough of these to fill a paper grocery bag. If you do, you will need to study these in very careful detail. For now focus on getting a feel for these documents and becoming comfortable admitting that they exist. Look through and read each and every one of these communications. When you do, ask yourself:

1. What is this bill for and is it correct?
2. Why was this bill not paid or paid on time? Did you forget about it? Did you not have the money?
3. How much do you owe? Is this amount correct?
4. Who do you owe? Do you owe the company who sold you the good or service or has this been transferred to a collection agency?
5. What fees or interest are being generated by not paying this bill?

The questions that you asked as you went through all of the late notices and collection letters probably did not make you feel good. That is alright. This is not going to be a fun process. Taking responsibility rarely is. However, it is a necessary step to taking care of these bills and being free of them forever. Remember, a little pain now will result in a lot of pleasure and freedom down the road. I did it and I am confident that you can too.

1.4 Summing Up Your Debt

Good Debt vs. Bad Debt.

It is entirely possible that you are a debt free individual. However, in today's society this is not very likely. You, like many Americans may have six maxed out credit cards, a home equity loan, a mortgage, car payment etc. You may feel like you are drowning in debt.

To become financially independent, you are going to need to sum up and eliminate any <u>unnecessary</u> debt. Now this brings up an interesting question. Just what is necessary debt? Necessary debt is debt that provides for the necessities of life or debt that provides a return on investment greater than the interest cost. I will explain both.

The average American home now costs well over $200,000. Few people have this money just sitting in the bank. That means that few people can just afford to pay cash for a house outright. Most of us, and I am no exception, will need to finance their first home purchase. This is OK. The alternative is that we continue to pay rent forever. This is not a good idea. When we rent something, we do not gain any equity in the house and are essentially throwing that money away. Purchasing a house with financing, while we do pay interest, allows us to put our money toward something. If you pay $1,000 as a mortgage payment, maybe $250 will be interest. However, the other $750 pays off part of the loan meaning that you now own $750 more of your house and you are worth $750 more. You are essentially saving money by borrowing. If you pay $1,000 in rent, you just pay $1,000 in rent.

Another "good debt" that will be of less interest throughout this book, is investment debt. Another example will be helpful.

Say you get a once in a lifetime opportunity to buy your Uncle Bob's business. It is very successful and you are guaranteed to make money. He wants $500,000 for it and you will make $1,000,000 your first year. You do not have $500,000 so you borrow and buy the business. After one year you have paid off the $500,000 and made $500,000 for yourself. Without having borrowed the money you would not have been able to make any money. That debt was necessary and positive.

Student loans are another example of investment debt. You are essential investing in your education in the hope that you will increase your earning potential down the road.

Now that we know what "good debt" is, we can also tell what "bad debt" is. Bad debt is any debt to finance an item that does not save you money, like a mortgage does, or make you money, like a business does. Examples of "bad debt" are car loans, appliance loans, or credit card balances. These types of debt do not save or make any money and only cost you in the form of interest.

Summing Up Your Bad Debt

Sit down and make a list of every bad debt that you carry. On this list you should write down the following for each debt.

1. Who you owe including name, address and phone number
2. How much money you owe
3. The current interest rates for these debts
4. Your monthly payments
5. The term of the loan (This is how long the loan is for)

Once you have done this for each debt you have, add them all up. This is your unnecessary debt load. One of your goals in the next chapter should be to get this number to zero.

Determine Your Net Worth

You should also determine you net worth. This can be a very important indicator of your overall financial health. Essentially, your net worth is the dollar value of everything you own minus the dollar value of all your debt. The easiest way to figure out this number is to sit down and list your assets and debt.

The following chart will give you a good idea of a net worth calculation. In the chart you will see that this person has a total asset value of $29,500 and a total debt owed of $177,500.

<u>Assets</u>	<u>Value</u>	<u>Debts</u>	<u>Value</u>
Car	$4,500	Credit Cards	$10,000
Stocks	$7,500	Mortgage	$150,000
Home Equity	$15,000	Student Loans	$10,000
Cash in Bank	$2,500	Car Loan	$7,500
Total	$29,500	**Total**	$177,500

To determine the total net worth of this person we subtract debts from assets, or:

$29,500 - $177,500 = <u>-$148,000</u>

The underlined result is this person's net worth. Their net worth at this point in time is **negative** $148,000. This means they owe $148,000 more than they have.

It is entirely possible when you first calculate your net worth, it will be negative. To make your net worth positive should be one of your goals.

Conclusion

This chapter was about gaining the knowledge you will need to make educated decisions with this information in later chapters. If you have carried out the instructions contained in the preceding pages, you have a fairly intimate understanding of your finances at this point in time. Knowing the state of your finances is the first step on the road to financial empowerment and freedom. This book will not ask you to examine these documents further. However, the steps that you have just taken should be repeated each month as part of your efforts. Just as before collect your documents over the month. At the end of the month, spend some time examining them. As your knowledge and familiarity increase you will need to spend less time to maintain a current understanding.

In the next chapter we will discuss goals and budgeting. In that chapter you will take the information we have gathered here and make some decisions on where you need to focus your efforts.

Chapter 2
Budgeting & Setting Goals

In Chapter 1, you gathered all of your financial documents for a one month period and looked them over. This was really just to get a good grasp for your particular financial status and resources. In this chapter, all that information will be formally summarized in an official budget. After all this information is correct and properly organized we will interpret that information and discuss setting goals. Finally, in this chapter we will discuss methods to take greater control of your money and financial matters.

2.1 Budgeting

You explored your costs in Chapter 1. Now we are going to total up and analyze all of those costs up in a monthly budget. This monthly budget will tell you, in detail, your total monthly expenses as well as where that money is going in stark black and white. If you can type this out on a computer, that is great. However, if you do not have access to a computer, pen and paper will do just fine.

Example 2.1 is a simple monthly budget plan format that you can easily copy. This budget example is divided into three parts. The first part is the income section. In this part of the budget, all sources of income are summed up. Part two of the budget is the expense section. Most people have many more expense categories than sources of income so this is the largest part of the budget. Lastly, in the third part we do a little math. Firstly we subtract your total costs from your total income and determine your disposable income. Disposable income is income that is not allocated to any bills and can be used as you see fit. It would be ideal if you saved this money.

To construct your budget, copy the format listed in Example 2.1. Copy down on paper or in your computer, all of the categories. Next, fill in the dollar amounts of your personal situation. For example, if your monthly income is $2,800 you would enter that amount where it says $3,000 in the sample budget. If one of the categories is not relevant to your situation, for example, property taxes when you own no property simply enter $0.

To calculate the "Percent of Cost" for a particular item, you will need to divide the dollar value of that category by the "Total

Expenses" value at the end of Part II of the budget and multiply by 100.

Example 2.1: A Monthly Budget
Part I: Income

Category	Amount
Wages or Salary	$3000.00
Income From Interest	$75.00
Investment Income	$0.00
Other Income	$0.00
Total Income	**$3075.00**

Part II: Expenses

Category	Monthly Cost	Percent of Costs
Housing		
Mortgage or Rent	$750.00	29.3%
Homeowner/Renter Insurance	$16.00	.6%
Property Taxes	$0.00	0%
Home Repairs	$0.00	0%
Home Improvement	$0.00	0%
Car Expenses		
Car Payments	$205.00	8%
Gas	$125.00	5%
Maintenance	$30.00	1.2%
Auto Insurance	$105.00	4.1%
Food		
Groceries	$125.00	5%
Dining Out	$100.00	4%
Snacks On The Go (e.g. Lattes)	$50.00	2%

Utilities

Electricity	$72.00	2.8%
Gas	$0.00	0%
Water	$18.00	.7%
Sewer & Garbage	$35.00	1.4%
Cable	$49.00	2%
Internet	$39.00	1.5%

Medical

Medical Insurance	$75.00	3%
Monthly Prescriptions	$35.00	1.4%
Fitness Club Dues	$0.00	0%
Misc. Expenses e.g. Co-pays	$0.00	0%

Family Responsibilities

Child Support	$0.00	0%
Alimony	$0.00	0%
Day Care	$0.00	0%
Tuition	$150.00	5.9%

Debt Payments

Credit Cards	$300.00	11.7%
Student Loans	$0.00	0%

Savings

Automatic Savings Plan	$0.00	0%

Entertainment

Vacations	$100.00	4%
Going Out(e.g. movies, clubs)	$100.00	4%
Hobbies	$0.00	0%

Misc. Expenses

Clothing	$50.00	2%
Toiletries	$25.00	1%

| Total Expenses | $2554.00 |

Part III: Summary

Total Income	$3075.00
Total Expenses	$2554.00
Income Minus Expenses	$521.00
Total Disposable Income	$521.00
Percent Of Income Considered Disposable	17%

Analyzing Your Budget

Once you have summarized all of your monthly money matters in a budget, you should again study these numbers.

If you have not already realized it, this book is going to require you to become intimately comfortable with studying, and interpreting numbers.

Look over each row and decide if the amount of money you are spending on a particular category is appropriate. By this I mean two things. One, are you spending what is considered to be the "normal" amount on an item? For example, if you are spending $500 a month on your car insurance, you are spending too much. Secondly, does the amount you are spending, seem reasonable to you? For example, if you are spending $500 a month going out, you are spending way too much on this activity. Some people may not consider this to be a problem, however, if you are reading this book we already know that you are interested in lowering your spending, saving and investing more, and ultimately reaching financial freedom. Look over your numbers now and give them some thought. Which numbers leap out at you?

Next, I want you to look through your budget and determine which monthly expenses can be altogether eliminated. Some cannot be eliminated. Obviously you are going to continue to eat and need water. However, some can be completely gotten rid of. Looking at our example budget, two immediately leap out. These are credit card payments and car payments. You may be asking yourself, "How can I stop paying those?". Well, you really can't just stop paying them, however, you can make changes to your lifestyle that will eliminate these. For example, if you sell your car, pay off your loan and using whatever cash you have on hand, buy another car, you will no longer have a car payment. If you stop using your credit cards and work hard to pay off any balance, suddenly you will not have any credit card payments. In addition, you will not be paying any more interest charges each month to boot. These savings can be used to increase positive categories such as "Automatic Savings Plan" which in turn increase other positive categories like "Interest Income". As you can see, by making a little lifestyle change you can already save and earn more money.

Along with categories that can be eliminated, I want you to look through your budget and find categories whose expenses can be reduced. Look through what you have spent over the last month on such categories as:

- Movies
- Eating Out
- Vacations
- Snacks
- Clothing
- Cable

I want you to seriously consider how you can reduce these costs. For example, limit yourself to going out to dinner or a movie once a week. Reconsider that new clothing purchase. Do you really need it? Eliminate those premium cable channels. Ask yourself if you need that croissant each morning. In the following section on goals, you should strongly consider setting a goal to reduce all of these expenses. These are not necessities, but only luxuries. In Chapter 3, we will explore the idea of luxuries in detail when we discuss radical spending controls.

Keeping Your Budget Current

Your monthly budget should be an ongoing process. Just as you are supposed to look at your bills and statements each month, sit down and update your budget. This will keep you completely up to date with your finances. In addition to keeping your knowledge current, you will be able to see what progress you are making in meeting your goals.

2.2 Goals

Setting Realistic Goals

Hopefully, by following the instructions in Chapter 1, you discovered problems that may exist in your financial life. This is the section where we make some realistic goals about these problems.

You may have simple problems such as not saving enough money. On the other hand, you may have larger problems such as a $50,000 credit card debt. No matter what your problem is, the first step to solving it is to identify it and decide how you would like to handle it. If you need to save more, simply make your goal to save more. If you are $50,000 in debt, make your goal to become debt free.

Your particular situation will determine what goals you set, but you will need to make them realistic. If you are not realistic with your goals you are only setting yourself up for failure and discouragement down the road.

For example, if you decide to save all of your income other than what you pay in bills, you will leave yourself with no spending money. This is unrealistic and you will find it almost impossible to maintain this goal. Likewise, if you set your goal of being debt free in 1 year when you have $50,000 in credit card debt and you make $30,000 a year you will also not be successful.

Keep your simple and manageable. If you need to save more, say you wish to save 20% of your income. If you are in debt, try to reduce your debt by 15% each year, or set your goal to be debt free in 5 years. You will find that simple, well thought out objectives are easier to accomplish and your success periodically will only reinforce your desire to see the goal through.

You should also write your goals down. This way you can refer back to them later and see how you are doing. Goals that are not written down have a nasty habit of being forgotten.

Suggested Goals

In the following paragraphs you will find many suggested goals. These are **ALL** goals that I set for myself when I was digging out of debt and starting to build my wealth. I would strongly suggest that these be your goals as well. Remember, only through discipline and determination, not to mention sacrifice, can you become financially independent and debt free.

Save More Money

No matter what your financial situation, you should make saving more one of your goals. Without money in the bank to protect you in hard times, you will often find yourself in trouble. Without savings, goods and services will cost you more as you will often have to finance them. Financing means interest and interest payments mean less money in your bank accounts. Saving money will be discussed in detail in a later chapter, however, for now get used to the idea of needing to save more.

Dig Out Of Debt

Now that you are finished with your budget, you can see how much your credit card payments are each month. A large portion of these payments is interest, unless you do not carry a balance. This ties up money that you need for savings and investment. Eliminating these payments and freeing yourself from credit card headaches will be essential to your success. This is not to say close all your credit card accounts. In fact DO NOT DO THAT! This can cause many more problems. Many credit card companies will greatly increase your interest rate if you close your account with a balance. Also if you have bad credit, you may not be able to replace these cards if you wish to repair your credit in the future. All I am saying is that if you do not carry a balance, you will have fewer bills and lower expenses and can redirect that money to more useful and beneficial efforts.

Eliminate Your Car Payment

Many Americans drive more than they need or can afford. How and why do they do this? Well, they finance everything and they drive the car for vanity in many cases. I can admit that it feels good to get everyone's attention when you drive up in a brand new expensive car. However, this costs you a lot. You have monthly interest payments each month. These draw down the money that you have available to save and invest. Free up more money by getting rid of these monthly payments. How to do this will be discussed in the next chapter.

Find A Roommate

You might like your privacy. We all do. When I first moved out on my own, I decided that I would finally have a place all to myself. I decided that I would live alone. This was all well and good until I needed to pay the rent.

My first apartment cost me $685 dollars a month plus utilities. That meant that I was paying close to $900 each month for my household. Now I had rented a two bedroom, two bathroom apartment with plenty of extra space that could have easily accommodated another person. However, I was stubborn. I liked having my office (which I mainly used to play video games) and I did not want to grow accustomed to the habits of another person, so every month I struggled with the rent and saved nothing.

I, again, was young and stupid. I did not ever sit down to think about the economics of sharing my living space. Let's look just how stupid I was. With all my extra space, I could have easily gotten a roommate and continued to live in the apartment that I had rented. That would have lowered the amount I paid to rent by $342.50 right off the bat. In addition, a roommate would have paid for half of all the utilities as well. All told, I could have saved myself about $450 a month, or $5400 a year just for putting up with another person in my space. That is an enormous cost saving that would have helped me dig out of debt faster, and save more quickly. However, again, I was young and stupid and I did not get a roommate. If you are looking to cut costs, give this one some serious thought as it can save you a bundle.

Spend Less

When you added up all of your non-essential purchases you may have been alarmed at how much you spend. Maybe, like me, you had never considered your spending habits until you added them all up and saw them in black and white.

I am not telling you to spend nothing and live like a hermit. After all, the purpose of this book is to provide yourself with the financial freedom and resource to truly enjoy life. However, you may want to carefully consider all of your purchases before making them and ask yourself; "Do I really need this?"

In the sunroom of my house, you will find a sheepskin rug. I spent $200 on this rug. It was a stupid impulse purchase of an item I did not need or even really want. I just fell in love with its novelty value. I did not reconsider the purchase before I spent my money and today that rug sits as a silent reminder to always think wisely before spending my money.

Use Your Plastic Less

In conjunction with a goal of spending less, you may wish to try and use your credit and debit cards less. A strategy for an all cash existence will be discussed in the following chapter.

Build An Investment Portfolio

You may wish to plan to let your money make more money for you. This is a great goal. An investment portfolio can build your personal wealth and prepare you for retirement all in one shot.

There are many steps that need to be taken to make sure that you are strong enough financially to begin an investment portfolio. These will be discussed in this book to some detail. Until that time, however, there is no reason that you cannot begin to plan for then now. A great place to start is simply by reading the business section of your local newspaper. Get familiar with the headlines and know what is going on in the world of business. That way, once you have learned how to invest and have the money to do so, you will also have a good working knowledge to start with.

Cut Your Costs

You may be spending more than you like to each month. This means that you are having to work more and are able to spend, save or invest less than you would like. One good goal might be to lower these costs. If you have more apartment than you need, you may consider moving to a smaller, cheaper unit. You may consider trading in your car and losing the auto loan for something you can buy outright. Several less drastic strategies may be to lower your electricity bill or maybe cancel your cable service. Do you really need 50 premium channels? What about that storage space you rent each month? Do you really need everything that is in there? Why not have a garage sale or consider donating some of the items in there to charity? You could turn some junk into cash or help out a charity and at the same time you eliminate a monthly rental bill.

Eliminate Some Luxuries

I have already mentioned eliminating some of those premium cable channels as a means to cut your monthly expenses. Along with premium cable channels there may be many luxuries that you consume each month. Each one by itself may not seem like it costs a lot of money, however, added up these can quickly save you a good amount of cash.

Take smoking for example. A pack of 20 cigarettes cost somewhere around $5 depending on where you live. If you smoke a pack a day, you are spending $35 a week and $1820 a year for this habit. If you put this money into an interest bearing account at 5% for 30 years, at the end you will have almost $127,000!

Smoking is by no means the only luxury, that you can reduce, if not eliminate. Drinking, dining out, the morning latte, the weekly magazines, your monthly massages, etc. can all be considered as places to save you a little money.

Now, I need to add a point. I am not telling you to live like a monk. I sincerely want you to enjoy your life. I do not mean that you can never partake in any of these activities. People like to eat out and I love a massage every now and again. All I am saying is that you can reduce these activities and save a bundle of money. Eat out only once a week. Try cutting down to a pack of cigarettes every other day. Only have a latte on those rough Monday mornings. Limit yourself to two drinks when you are out with friends. A little effort can be greatly rewarding.

Any Other Goal That You Deem Fit

In the preceding pages, I listed a number of ideas of goals for you to save money, increase your savings and improve your financial situation. However, only you are intimately involved with your situation. Only you know all of your habits and ways. You will really be the best person to set goals for yourself. I want you at this point to give some very serious, very honest thought to your financial situation. I want you to try and decide on a few other ideas to save money, invest more, and to spend less. Remember to keep your goals realistic and to set yourself up for success. Start out small and go bigger from there. At first, maybe save a hundred dollars a week. When you are comfortable with that level, try moving to $200 and so on.

Conclusion

In this chapter we went over the basics of budgeting and goal setting. These two subjects are only second in importance to admitting there is a problem with your finances. Without monthly budgeting there is no way to track your improvements over time and keep track of your progress. Make sure that you adhere to a monthly budgeting schedule. I cannot stress this enough. Without this, you will only spin your wheels and become frustrated, sliding backwards away from financial freedom.

Goals are also extremely important. Without proper goal setting, you will have no way to focus your efforts. I have said it many times in this chapter, but I want to say it once more just to drive it home. Keep your goals realistic and manageable. Start small and expand and increase them as you become more disciplined.

In the next chapter, we will discuss a number of ways to cut your living expenses and ways to put the breaks on unnecessary spending. These are the tools to help you reach your goals.

Chapter 3
Cost Cutting & Increasing Your Income

At this point, you should be very well acquainted with your particular financial situations and any shortcomings you may possess. Most likely, to improve your finances we are going to need to eliminate your debts, save more money and invest as much as possible. This chapter is going to provide you with many of the tools to do just that. First we will discuss how to lower your monthly costs simply, without depriving yourself of the joys of life. Secondly, we will discuss several safeguards that you can put in place to help you manage your money more efficiently.

3.1 Consumerism Run Amok

When we eat food we consume it. In economic terms consuming is the use of manufactured goods and services in a manner that does not result in further goods and services. For example, when you eat a loaf of bread many inputs went into that loaf of bread. The farmer bought grain to sow, used fertilizer, etc. The baker bought the flour, added eggs and used heat from natural gas to bake it. The store you bought it from used the services of a trucking company to move the bread from the baker to their shelves. You however, bought the bread to eat. You are not going to make a further product with the bread and are only going to consume it.

We are all consumers. We eat food, drive cars, and buy televisions and DVDs. We also consume services like cable channels, internet service, and auto repair. There is nothing wrong with being a consumer.

There is also a phenomenon called consumerism. Consumerism is associating your happiness with the acquisition of goods. How often have you heard the term shopaholic? This term, often jokingly, is used to describe someone who shops for fun. They do not need the items they buy, they simply want them and enjoy the act of buying new things. Having them makes them happy. Not everyone suffers from consumerism, but many do. You might.

Avoiding the pitfalls of consumerism can be difficult. You will need to fight your consumerist urges in your battle to find financial freedom. You should only buy what you truly need or want. No, again, I do not want you to give up every modern convenience. What I am saying is that I want you to truly consider and plan for your expenditures. Remember that sheepskin rug I talked about? That was a personal instance where I suffered from consumerism. I did not want the rug, I simply wanted to buy it. As another example of what I mean I want you to consider cell phones. Today, mobile phones are everywhere . Most of the readers of this book will have one. However, how many of you upgrade your cell phone frequently (more than once every two years)? If you do not, I am quite certain that you know someone who does. Why do you or they do that? If you ask, you will frequently hear reasons like:

- It has the new camera
- It is so much smaller
- I can watch TV on it
- I can listen to music on it
- It has GPS
- It's so much cooler than what I have now
- It comes in blue

The buyers of these devices are suffering from consumerism. They do not need all the latest bells and whistles. They want the latest phone so they can be the envy of friends and peers. They may be attracted to the latest features and will not make use of them. In many cases, like playing music, they already have a device that does that and will now have two. Well you still only have two ears right?

As you are reading this book and as you are out in the world spending your hard earned money (never forget that you have to work to get it) I want you to consider at each purchase, the following questions:

1. Do I really need this item?
2. Am I buying this item because I need it or for what people will think of me for having it?

If you consider these questions and remember what I wrote about being honest with yourself, I am quite certain you can avoid falling into a habit of consumerism.

3.2 Think In Terms Of A Year

The title of this section may seem a little cryptic but is actually a very simple idea. Few people will give much thought to a small amount. If you spend $5 dollars a day on lattes or $15 dollars a week on cigarettes, these seem like insignificant amount. No one is going to loose much sleep over these. However, if you consider these amounts in the context of the year they become more much substantial and it is much easier to care about these habits. For example, spending $5 a day each day for a year is actually the same as spending $1825 once that year. Spending $15 dollars a week on cigarettes adds up to $780! You may see how thinking in terms of a year will make you care more about saving even a dollar a day.

When you read through the cost cutting suggestions in the next section, the ideas may not seem like they will save you immediate big bucks. In fact, they won't. However, each of these little steps can add up to large costs savings over the course of the year. The same will be true of saving and investing in following chapters as well. A little at a time over a long period can add up to a very large number. Remember this.

3.3 Cut Your Costs

Not many people in the world can increase their income whenever they want. There are ways to increase your income through investment and these will be discussed in a later chapter. All that being said, it is far easier to use the income you do have more efficiently than it is to increase it. What follows in this section of the book are a number of ideas to do just that.

These ideas are ways that you can use your money more efficiently without giving up many things that you may enjoy. You are going to need to give up some things in this journey. For example, you can no longer max out your credit card buying cruises to the Caribbean. However, that does not mean you cannot vacation and it does not mean that you must sacrifice everything that you enjoy. Let's get started.

Eliminate Your Car Payment

This idea was hinted at in the preceding chapter. In this section we are going to explore my particular brand of car philosophy. With this mindset, you will be able to get rid of interest payments altogether and lower your insurance rates as well.

If you are like many people out there, you have an auto loan. Each month, you pay a certain amount to your lender against the loan. A certain amount of this goes to pay off the principal of the loan and a certain amount is interest. If you had no car loan, you would have no need to make any monthly payments. This money in turn could be used to pay off other debt or save more. In addition, many auto lenders require that the recipients of their loans carry comprehensive insurance. If you have no auto loan, you have the option to lower your monthly auto insurance bills as well by carrying liability coverage only[1]. With no auto loan, you then have the option to lower your insurance bill by carrying liability coverage only.

You may be asking yourself just how this can be accomplished. There are several ways in which you can eliminate your auto loan payment.

Firstly, you can pay off your existing loan. This is really a very easy idea. You can simply pay more each month for a shorter period of time. This will effectively shrink the duration of the loan and bring closer the day when the car is paid off. Try, for example, paying twice your monthly payment. See how quickly that will reduce the loan.

Now, there is something you should consider. There may be an early repayment penalty associated with your loan. You will need to explore this with your lender. This fee may be considerable, but is often less than the amount you would have paid in interest if you paid off your loan at the given rate.

If you are nowhere near paying off your loan, you may consider trading to a more economical (by that I mean a cheaper) vehicle. You will need to trade in or sell your vehicle first. Using what equity you have in the vehicle (equity is determined by taking the value of the vehicle minus what you owe on it) you can buy a car outright. With no loan, you will again, not have any monthly payments to worry about.

Keep Your Fuel Costs Low

Continuing with the theme of reducing your transportation costs, you should always keep your fuel costs as low as you can. It is never a wise idea to drive a big gas guzzling car unnecessarily. If you have a giant car that gets 10 miles to the gallon, you should consider trading it in for a more fuel efficient car.

In addition to a more fuel efficient vehicle, you can consider using mass transit if you live where this is available. The costs of fuel (not

---

[1] Discuss this option with your insurance agent to determine if this decision is appropriate to your specific situation.

to mention parking) can very quickly be reduced by using your city's subway or bus system.

You can always consider getting rid of your gym membership and buying a bicycle as well. Keep in shape and stop worrying about gas prices all in one move.

Keeping Things Maintained

Have you ever heard that an ounce of prevention is worth a pound of cure? This is true. It is often much cheaper to provide periodic maintenance than to deal with the fallout when things break down. This is true of cars, houses and even you!

Vehicle manufacturers recommend that you change your oil every 3000 miles. This is by far the simplest and cheapest way to ensure the health of your motor vehicle. You should always follow this guideline (not to mention making sure you have oil in your car to begin with). You can have this done at one of those innumerable drive-through lube shops or, you can cut costs even more, and learn to do it yourself.

Make sure all of your cars fluids are always where they should be when you change your oil as well. Also make sure that you keep up to date on maintenance your:

- Brakes
- Tires
- Air Filters
- Belts

Keeping yourself maintained is also of paramount importance in your quest to keep costs low. I used to be a procrastinator. I would avoid the doctor and dentist. I hated going. However, once I was forced to get a root canal, to the cost of over $2000, because I had failed to go in and get a cavity taken care of. The cavity filling would have costs a simple $200! Talk about penny wise and pound foolish!

Buy Generic

Many people look down on generic products from companies that they have never heard of. However, these products can be a very useful tool to save more money.

When you buy a brand name product, often times the price of the product reflects all of the advertising that was bought to promote the product. This means that you are paying for more than you really need. The generic product often has equal quality but a lower price.

This can be applied to any number of items that you may need. There are grocery stores that specialize in low cost generic products of equal quality to their higher priced competitors. Try these out and see how you can lower you monthly grocery bill.

Food is not the only category that generic items can save you money. Try buying generic clothes if you can. Why pay more money to advertise the company's logo for them for free? Generic drugs are becoming ever more common and popular as well. These are the same chemicals as name brand pharmaceuticals. They have the same government oversight and FDA approval as the name brands but are frequently lower in cost. If you are on prescription medicine, a simple conversation with your doctor or pharmacists could possibly save you quite a bit of money at your next refill.

Buy Used

It can be nice to have a brand new product. However, in your quest to save and invest more money, you should try and limit your purchases of new items and buy used when you can.

This idea can apply to any number of items. If you need a car, go to a used car lot or look in the classifieds. If you need clothes, yard equipment or electronics, try a second hand charity store. The items that you find at these vendors are frequently of very reliable quality with savings as much as 90%! These savings can really add up and can stretch your budget quite a bit. Purchases from charity stores also help support these organizations and their noble work.

Shop Around

Knowing who is selling an item you need and knowing what they charge is an important skill in reducing your monthly costs. This is true for just about anything that you will spend your money on. If you need a different apartment, find out what the apartments in the area are renting for and what amenities are available at what prices. If you need a new car (new to you that is), do not buy the first one you come across. Look at a few and don't ever feel rushed into making a purchase.

Some grocery stores are more expensive than others. They offer an attractive trendy environment and many people think they offer quality for higher prices. Truth be told, they sell the same food as the other store down they way with bright intrusive lighting, only with a 5% mark up. Save a few bucks and go for the store with the not so attractive and relaxing interior that has lower prices.

Also look for sales. Don't buy right away when you see a price quoted. Wait a week or two and see what happens to the price. Many stores will also match competitor coupons. If you find a store that has a lower price, but it will cost you $30 in gas to get there, take the advertisement into a local store and see if they will match the price. What is the worse they can say? No? Well in that case you can either not purchase the item or be forced to drive out to the other store. Either way, you are no worse off for asking.

Cut Your Entertainment Bills

Entertainment costs can quickly add up. These costs, however, can be controlled just like any other. Controlling these costs can free up large amounts of money for saving and investment.

Movies are an ever increasing cost. Evening movie tickets can easily cost between $10 and $14 depending on which movie theater you choose you go to and where you live. For a couple that can be almost $30 dollars in costs before you buy any popcorn! There are several ways to cut these costs down. Try going to only matinees. These are generally earlier in the day and are usually about 60% of the price of an evening ticket. You can also try going to second run theaters. These theaters show movies that are no longer in the top ten. These movie theaters operate on a business model that makes money from food and drink sales, not ticket prices. As a direct result, tickets at these theaters are generally only a few dollars. The savings from going to the cheaper movie theater and spending $6 instead of $28 is $22!

Another way to save money at the movie theater is to absolutely forbid yourself from buying any concessions in the theater. If you are one of those people who absolutely needs some snacks during a movie, you could always go to the store, buy some snacks at much lower prices and sneak them in. Most theaters forbid this and I do not recommend it. However, I do know it happens.

Staying in is another good way to limit your entertainment costs. Try renting a movie and having dinner while you watch it. Movie rentals are only about $3 these days and no one will prohibit snacks in your living room. To avoid pesky late fess, try one of the online video rental services. For less than $20 a month, you can rent unlimited movies through the mail. Postage is paid and you can keep the movies as long as you want. This way, nothing is ever late, and you fix the cost of your movie rentals for the month.

Cutting your cable bills by eliminating the premium channels or totally canceling your cable can be another great way to reduce your entertainment costs. Think about your viewing habits over the last month. How much cable did you actually watch? How much did you have to pay for this service? Was it worth it?

If you are an avid book buyer, try using your local library instead of buying every book that draws your fancy. These are free services generally provided by the county. You can have as many as 25 books checked out at once in some cases. That is enough to keep any bookworm busy for a while. If you happen to be a student, you can also take advantage of your schools library as well.

Avoid The One Armed Bandit

If you live in an American state these days, it is most likely that your state has some form of legalized gambling. Whether it be the lottery, Native American casinos, video poker, online poker, or a full blown casino resort strip, gambling can wind up costing you money that you do not need to spend.

Do not think of gambling as a means to get rich, an investment, or as a form of recreation. Think of gambling as a means to lose your money in a calculated, statistically predictable manner. Do yourself a favor and avoid the headache all together.

Watch Your Speed

I used to have a lead foot and I did not worry too much about speeding tickets. When I got them, I sometimes paid them. When I did not pay them, the fines only got bigger and I still did not worry about them. This was probably the stupidest thing I ever did. Not only was I digging myself in a deep hole financially, I was doing it with an organization (i.e. the government) who could take away necessary privileges such as driving.

Do not be the fool that I was. Avoid every type of ticket that you can. If you are already in financial trouble, you do not need the headache. If you are in a good financial position, why trouble yourself with the expense and trouble of tickets. Avoid problems by keeping your car registered, you lights working, don't run red lights, only use carpool lanes when you are allowed, use your turn signals, and most importantly WATCH YOUR SPEED!

Most of the times that I was cited for speeding, I was in a rush to get somewhere because I had not allowed sufficient time to get where I needed to go. Most of the time I was late for work. The simple way that I avoided the need to speed was to leave for work at a decent hour. I now leave every day 30 minutes before I really "have" to. This means that traffic problems or car trouble won't usually make me late. If I am late it is only <u>VERY</u> occasionally. Another added bonus to getting to work early is that you will appear to be a "go getter" to your boss. Maybe the next time a promotion is available (with a raise), they will think of you and your "always on time and eager" work habits.

Travel In The Off Season

You need to take vacations and enjoy the fruits of your labors. However, that being said, why not make your relaxing vacations as inexpensive as possible?

One of the best ways to do that is to travel in the off season. Off seasons vary by where you plan to go. In Europe, the off season is in the winter time. Now this period is the height of the season in the Caribbean. You will need to do some research and talk to friends, family and travel professionals about their travel experiences.

Another really good place to find inexpensive travel deals is in the "Travel" section of your local newspaper. Most likely this section is not printed daily so you will need to learn when it comes out. In these types of sections they often have listings of the cheapest airfares from your particular local airport as well as articles featuring far off destinations at reasonable prices.

Eliminate Unnecessary Costs

My first car was one of my most prized possessions when I was 18. I loved that car. I have lots of very pleasant memories associated with that car. However, like everything on this earth, that car aged and I needed to replace it. I did. I bought a newer, economical car. However, I did not really want to get rid of the old one. I had sentimental attachment to it. I did not have anywhere to put it. So I rented a parking space each month at a local mini-storage park. It cost me $35 a month.

What I bought for $35 a month was more time when I did not have to face the music and realize that I needed to part ways with my first car. I needed to just face facts and let it go. As far as the car was concerned it just sat there, rusting and becoming worth less money each month, and I was paying money for this! This was all very silly. I finally sold the car for practically nothing to free myself from the monthly rental bill.

It is very possible that if you look hard enough in your life, you will find something like this. You are paying money for a service that you do not need simply to avoid dealing with some unpleasant facts. Cut your costs by simply facing these facts and move on. You will be a happier person and your wallet will thank you.

Keep Your Energy Bills Low

Few people out there would argue that it is wise to leave televisions running when no one is home, to use the heat when it is 70 degrees outside, or to leave the window open when your AC is running. Most people would agree with this but a lot of them might be guilty of these actions.

Wasting energy that you pay for is the same as wasting money. Simply put, don't do it. Looking at how you and your family use energy can save you a lot of money. A few simple tips to save money on energy consumption are:

- Use cold water for your laundry.
- Don't leave lights, TVs, or radios on when no one is around
- Only use the heat when your house gets below 60 degrees.
- Only use the AC when your home gets above 80 degrees.
- Run the dishwasher only when it is full.
- Don't use central heating and AC if you have it. Instead try using a space heater or a single room AC in places like the bedroom.
- Don't leave your computer running all the time.

These are just a few simple ideas. I am sure that your local utility can provide you with extensive information on lowering your consumption (and your bills). Their phone number will always be listed on your monthly statement. Take advantage of it.

Additionally, if you own a home, you may qualify for federally funded home weatherizing programs. Information about these programs can be found at the website of US Department of Housing at http://www.hud.gov .

Moderation When On The Town

Many people like to go out after work and have a cocktail or two. There is nothing wrong with this. I myself enjoy going out with coworkers. It can be nice to unwind and compare notes about how the day panned out. However, those tabs at the bar can quickly add up to big bills.

You can go to the extreme route and give up drinking all together and just have a soda when you go out. However, this might not be the most popular of choices. Another way to go is to limit your expenses when at the bar. Try taking only cash when you go out. Don't take any plastic with you at all. That way, when you run out of cash, you are done. You can also try limiting yourself to a set number of drinks and then call it a night.

Is It Really Necessary?

Before you spend any money, you should always ask yourself if what you are buying is really necessary.

For example, say you just got into an accident in your car. It was not your fault and the insurance company has given you a check to repair the cosmetic damage to your car. For this example let us assume that the car is fine mechanically. Why should you go out and spend that money repairing your car? Why not put the money in the bank or better yet, an investment? Ignore the scratches and move on.

You can apply this philosophy to many areas or your life. Ignore little things that would otherwise costs lots of money and ask yourself "Should I really pay for this?"

3.4 Spending Controls

If you are reading this book, you probably already suspect that you have a problem controlling your spending habits and managing your money. Don't feel bad. I was exactly the same way. I knew that I needed to spend less money, but somehow it never worked out. What I figured out was that I needed to make it harder for me to spend my money and easier for me to control my spending in general. This section is all about how to force yourself to spend less. We will be discussing several techniques to put the brakes on your spending habits even if your will power is weak. Some of these tips may work for you and others may not. I have used all of these tricks at various times.

The basic idea here is to change your mindset about spending. However, this kind of thing does not change over night. The way you spend your money has been formed over all of the years of your life and it will take a little time to alter this. What these techniques do, is to automate the process of spending control while you change your habits and mindset. Essentially, these ideas take all of the thinking out of the equation and force you to accept limits. If this idea is a little fuzzy now, it will become more clear as you read through the following ideas.

Carrying Only Cash

One of the easiest ways to limit your spending is to only carry cash with you. If you do not have access to all of your savings in a convenient ATM/debit card you will not be able to spend any of that money. It doesn't matter how much you want that new stereo, if you do not have enough cash for it, you will not buy it.

This idea has some strong and weak points. First, this is a great way to make you think about your purchases. A lot of people (I am no exception) have trouble identifying transactions they carry out with their bank cards with money in the account. I don't know about you but I have always found it easier to spend $500 with a bank card then I have in handing over $500 in cash. Something about the cash just makes it harder to do. Also, in the past I have made a string of small purchases, say at a mall, with a bank card and not even realized I had just spent several hundred dollars and overdrawn my checking account. Handing over cash and watching as your wallet gets thinner will really bring home how much money you are spending.

In addition to being aware of all the money you are spending, paying with cash is a great way to force yourself to think about your purchases. An example might help.

Say that you are out and you see a nice new television set for $500. You only have $100 in cash on you and you carry no bank cards. You will have to go home, go to the bank and return to the store before you will be able to make this purchase. This will take some time. You might even have to go back to the store the next day after having slept on the purchase impulse. This will also get you out of the showroom, with their salespeople and give you a chance to quietly reflect on whether or not you need this purchase. Maybe in that time, you will think about buying a used television, maybe you will remember you already have a TV and it works fine. Maybe you will decide that you really do want to purchase the television. Anyway you slice it, you will be forced to think about and consider your purchase. If you do this, chances are, you will make smarter more thought out decisions.

There is a downside to only carrying cash that you will need to plan for. If all you carry is cash, your emergency money will be limited to what you have in your pocket. This means that you will need to give careful thought to how much money you may need at any point.

Allowances

In the previous section we talked about carrying and spending only cash. Limiting yourself to spending only cash is a great way to help save money and limit your purchases. However, I did not mention any way of limiting the cash you carry around. One idea for limiting the cash you carry around is to bring back something from your childhood- an allowance.

Give yourself a certain amount to spend each week. This amount should include all of the costs of your food, gas, entertainment, etc. to spend while you are out and about. This will be all the cash you can spend that week. Put the money in a pile somewhere. Do not keep a running total in your head and use the ATM when you need more. That will defeat the purpose of the cash allowance.

Again as your pile of money decreases, you will become aware of how much you are spending and what you are buying. When your pile of money is gone, you are done spending money for the week. Use some will power and do not let yourself have anymore money. After several weeks of doing this, your budgeting skills and self discipline will begin to quickly increase.

If you are uncomfortable carrying around large sums of money, you can take advantage of so-called "prepaid credit cards" that are not linked to your checking account. These cards can be found at most retailers that sell gift cards. You can also find these cards by entering "prepaid debit card" into an Internet search engine. In a nutshell, these cards act similarly to a debit card except they are not connected to a checking account. Instead, you load the card with money in advance from your bank account. There is a monthly fee that varies from card to card. Obviously, you will want to find the lowest fee you can.

You may be asking yourself, "why not just use a debit card?". The answer is two-fold. Firstly, if you are using a debit card, you have access to all of the money in your checking account and you may use more than your allowance. This would defeat the goal of setting a weekly allowance. Secondly, you cannot overdraw a prepaid credit card. Avoiding overdraft fees will more than make up for the monthly service fee for using the card.

Bank Inconveniently

Many banks try to lure new customers with the promise of convenient access to their money. This can be a great asset in a bank if you are a disciplined spender and are in control of your finances. If you have trouble controlling yourself, like I did, this can be a headache. When I did not have any self control regarding my finances, access to my money was the last thing I needed. My bank account rarely had any money in it and I would clean it out and most likely overdraw it when I did.

To solve this problem, I decided to make access to my money much harder. To do so, I went out and sought financial institutions that were anything but convenient. What I ultimately decided to use were brokerage firms and brokerage accounts. As, I have said before, I would buy money orders with my cash each night. The next day, I would then send these money orders to my brokerage account in the mail. The actual process of depositing the money would often take in excess of 7 days. This was OK. I did not want immediate access to it. Also, the fact that I did not see these accounts on a daily basis helped me to remove them from my mind.

To remove money from these accounts, say for an unforeseen expense, I would call and request a check. This would take another 3 days or so. Not a terribly long time, but long enough to allow me to consider what I was spending the money on. I would then cash the check at my local bank where I had my checking account.

This setup allowed me to control my money to a much larger degree than I had been able to in the past. Eventually I got used to not spending my money and thinking of the bank as off limits. I no longer use brokerage accounts in this way, but they were very helpful in getting me to this point.

One downside that I do want to mention about this setup was fees. Brokerage accounts are not intended to e places to store you cash. The firms that provide these accounts want you to make purchases of stocks and bonds. To discourage people from using their accounts in the way I have just described, brokerage firms often charge fees when you do not make a stock purchase over a three month period. These fees can be up to $35 dollars. This was expensive, but for me the lack of access to my money was worth the fee.

3.4 Ideas For Increasing Your Income

Work More Hours

If you are a person who is paid by the hour, working more hours means you make more money. There is no reason that you cannot volunteer to pick up extra hours. Here are a few ways that you can do this:

- Help cover for sick coworkers
- Cover while people are on vacation
- Volunteer for late night shifts
- Tell your boss you would like to work more and see if they will give you another shift

Many companies during crunch seasons (accountants at tax time, the post office at Christmas, electric companies during summer, restaurants during summer) will gladly allow you to work overtime as well to make sure that their customers are taken care of. Not only does this mean more hours of work and pay, but a higher overtime rate of pay as well. Work as many of these shifts as you can find.

Take on a Second Job

We all work hard. However, sometimes it is just not enough. If your job does not pay you enough and for one reason or another you cannot or will not leave it, try picking up a second job. You can find a second job on part time basis if you are already working full time somewhere else.

One type of job that you may want to consider is working "Student Jobs". These types of jobs are often part time, maybe 25 hours a week. These jobs also do not occur 9-5. So, if you are already employed during those hours, you can easily add one of these into your schedule.

Work Temporarily

Many companies will need people for limited periods of time only. Accountants need extra people to answer the phones at tax time and shippers need extra handlers during the holiday season. If you have a particular skill set that is relevant to these companies, there is no reason that you cannot take on a second job on a temporary basis.

If this idea appeals to you, you can also sign up with temporary agencies. These companies make a business out of matching up employers and employees who can benefit from each other. The employer pays the agency a fee for this service. There are many different types of temp employment agencies out there. I know of specific agencies that handle medical professionals, restaurant workers and industrial workers.

Sign up with one of these companies in advance and they will call you when they have jobs that need filling. If the job works with your schedule you can take it and earn a little extra money. If it does not, you can pass and they will call you next time they have a job. You have nothing to lose.

Ask For A Raise

This option may not be very successful and I am only throwing it out there for thoroughness, but you can always ask your boss for a raise. If you do choose this option, think things through carefully before preceding. Make a list of all the reasons that you deserve a raise. Do not simply say, "I need more money". You will need to convince your boss that you are worth the extra money because of what you offer the company, not on the basis of your personal needs.

Conclusion

In this chapter, we have discussed a variety of techniques to limit your expenses and put the brakes on your spending habits. These two ideas form the backbone of the spending philosophy laid out in this book and represent the biggest two steps you can take to finding financial independence. If you dedicate yourself to these two goals, you will find that you have more money in you bank accounts to save and invest, eliminate the need to borrow, protect you from financial emergencies and enjoy life.

Chapter 4
Eliminate Your Debt

Debt is an epidemic that our country is suffering from. It is our drug of choice. In our efforts to keep up appearances, keep up with the Joneses, and have the latest and greatest stuff, our country has developed a negative savings rate. What that means is that as a country, we spend more than we make. This is all made possible by debt and borrowing. I was certainly no exception to this rule. At my low point, I had six maxed out credit cards. I still have very little idea what all that debt bought me. You may be the same way. You may know exactly what you have bought but still have problems dealing with your debt. Any way you slice it, this chapter is all about how to eliminate your debt and free yourself financially.

Rainy Day Fund

Many people live paycheck to paycheck. I was certainly one of those people. I used to have a plan the day before payday, of how I was going to spend each and every penny of my paycheck. We were paid on Fridays and by Saturday or Sunday, most of the money was gone. If this sounds familiar to you, don't feel bad, you are not alone. As a result of this, many people do not have any kind of savings. If you have no savings, you have no financial cushion and the smallest financial disaster, like a broken timing belt or a dead battery in your car, can leave you high and dry with nowhere to turn.

This section of the book is all about how to set up a rainy day fund. We are going to talk about how much you will need to set aside and when you should use it.

Essentially, a rainy day fund is a financial first aid kit. It is meant to deal with unforeseen problems that could become big problems if not treated quickly and effectively. If you do not have a rainy day fund and manage to pay off your credit cards, a little emergency can force you to max them out again. This fund will greatly increase the odds of breaking that cycle.

For a rainy day fund, you should have three months living expenses. To find out how much you should have in a rainy day fund, look at the budget you prepared after reading Chapter 2. Find your total monthly expenses and multiply that number by three. This should provide you with a good cushion in the event that you lose your job, are injured, have car trouble, etc.

To actually set up your fund, you should open a bank account. It is not wise to keep several thousand dollars lying around in cash.

Houses get robbed, roommates steal, and fires do happen. One little disaster like that can have you back in square one. You need to avoid this at all costs. The type of bank account you need to open should keep your money as cash. Types of accounts that would be ideal are checking, savings and money market accounts. Do not lock up your money in accounts such as certificates of deposit or in investments. After all, the purpose of this money is to be used in an emergency. The last thing you need is a dead car and someone telling you that you cannot have your money. For specifics on each of these types of accounts, refer to "Chapter 5: Saving". If you are not able to open a bank account due to poor personal credit, there are suggestions on where to keep your money in the following chapter as well.

Now, it is not wise to ignore all of your bills and fill up a rainy day fund. All this will accomplish is to burden you with many additional fees and interest charges. You need to keep up with your bills as best you can and set aside extra money when possible. This may not be easy. In fact this may be hard especially if your personal money habits were as bad as mine were. However, think of this as your first step in taking control of your finances and working actively to better your life. It may be hard at first but it will get easier and more rewarding. Remember "No pain, no gain!".

Identifying Your Creditors

In the first chapter of this book, you explored your personal situation to some degree and began to seriously look at your debt. Now is the point where you sit down and make a list of all the companies to which you owe money. This is going to be a very important list so it would be a good idea to go out and buy a file folder to keep it and all the other documents this effort will generate neat and orderly.

If you have been continuing to keep your financial papers in order you should have all of your bills, collection notices, and letters from creditors in a file or box somewhere. Take these, sit down and read **ALL** of them. Make sure that a current copy of your credit report from each of the three credit bureaus is in this stack. You need to look through each of these papers for debts that are outstanding and accounts that are past due. You do not need to concern yourself with your monthly cable bill. That is a recurring charge and if it is up to date, does not fit into the category of debt. What you are looking for are debts that are late or debts that are accruing interest charges. Examples of this type of debt are:

- Credit card debt
- Student loans
- Car loans
- Used lines of credit
- Store specific financing. For example $800 in financed appliances at a local retailer.
- Medical/dental bills
- Payday loans or advances
- Past due tax bills
- All late bills
- Any accounts in collections
- Charge off accounts. These occur when an account is closed with a negative balance. For example, an overdrawn bank account.
- Past due utility bills from when you moved

This is only a short list of some of the types of debt that you may have. Each of these types of debts will cost you money each month in interest payments. This is money that could be in your bank account *earning* you interest! You need to make it a goal to eliminate ALL of this debt.

One category that you may have noticed was absent from this list was your mortgage. Mortgages are a special kind of debt that permit you to gain wealth and eliminate rent payments.

Now make a list of each debt that you find. Make sure that each entry on the list has the following information:

- Name of the creditor
- Address of the creditor
- Phone number of the creditor
- Amount that is owed
- Interest rate being charged

- Original purpose of the debt. Was it for school, a boat, etc.?
- Past due or current

With this information on each and every debt that you find, you will have a great road map for eliminating your debt.

Monitoring Your Credit File

If every creditor has sent you a paper bill and you have gone through and read all of those as suggested in the previous section, you are in good shape and know who all of your creditors are. Unfortunately, creditors are not always the most organized of companies and can have communication problems like anyone else. They may not have sent you a bill in the mail because of an error on their part. They may have used an old address. A creditor may have an incorrect phone number. There are lots of reasons that they may not have been able to communicate with you. This does not mean that you do not owe anything. It is very possible that a creditor has not successfully communicated with you via mail or the telephone but may have added a record to your credit file.

This last fact means that, in your effort to eliminate your debt you should, again, make a habit of examining your credit file. A simple way to do this is with a credit monitoring service. For a small monthly fee, you can examine your entire credit file with your credit score. In this file, you will see your debts and who claims that you owe them money. The important thing is that they will have their contact information listed and this will allow you to move ahead with your debt repayment.

Before signing up with a credit monitoring service, know that they are not all created equally. Many of them offer access to only one of the three credit bureaus and may not offer a credit score. Without knowing what is in all three files you can never see the whole picture. To that end make sure that you sign up for a service that offers a "Three Bureau Report" and a "Three Bureau Credit Score". For $9.95 a month this service provides all of the bits of information that I need and provides email updates in the event of a new record being added to my credit file. I subscribe to one of these services and it is well worth it.

No New Debt and Hard Choices

You need to make it a priority to generate no new debt while you are trying to eliminate your debt load. This is important for two reasons. Firstly, you will not be getting ahead if you run up a credit card just as soon as you pay it off. Secondly, forcing yourself to break you reliance on credit and refocus your emergency planning around savings instead will begin to positively alter your mindset and develop spending discipline.

I am not telling you to starve if you have no food or not repair your car when it breaks down. That would be stupid. If you are in a jam and have no other way to dig out than to use a credit account, do it. I just want you to be sure that no other alternatives exist before you proceed and that you are making wise, educated decisions.

A great way to begin to dig out of debt is to incorporate debt repayment into your monthly budget. Again, a spending plan laid out in black in white has an odd way of compelling you to abide by it and follow the plan. Set aside a certain amount of money each month to both your rainy day fund and your debt repayment. There is no reason you cannot build your emergency cushion and eliminate your debt simultaneously.

Unfortunately, there will be times when you may be faced with more bills than you have money in your budget to pay. This is an unfortunate scenario and will make you feel pretty bad about yourself. If you are reading this book and following the plan, you should be beginning to feel personal responsibility towards your debts and a burning desire to be free from debt forever. You may be tempted to invade your rainy day fund to pay for these bills. Before deciding to use your rainy day fund to pay off a past due bill, you need to ask yourself what the bill is for and you need to remember why you have a rainy day fund. You need to ask yourself if the bill is for an essential service such as water, gas, or electricity, that you will have trouble living without. If it is for a service that meets these criteria, pay the bill. You need to make sure you have what you need to live. If however, the bill is for a credit card that is maxed out from when you went on that shopping spree, you should make sacrifices to other areas of your budget such as entertainment to pay for it, but leave your emergency fund for emergencies. If an emergency ever comes along, you will be glad then for your discipline now.

Contacting Your Creditors & Paying Your Debts

Once you have a rainy day fund set up, know who your creditors are, and have budgeted money to begin paying off your debts, you are ready to begin contacting your creditors and making arrangements to pay them.

Now, most people out there think that they need to pay off their debts in the full amount. If your accounts are current, this is a good idea as it will protect your credit rating. A good credit rating is a great asset to have and is difficult to get back once it's gone. However, if your debts are already past due or in collections, you have other options to lower your debt load.

If Your Debts Are Current...

If your debts are current, you should do your best to keep them current and to protect your credit rating. Staying current, protecting your credit and paying down your debt can be a hard thing to accomplish. It can be done, however. What follows are several options that can help you accomplish just that.

Keep Your Accounts Open!

I have not used punctuation in any of the subchapter topics to this point until now. I do this because closing their accounts is one of the first things a person in financial trouble will do. The idea behind it is simple. If you get rid of your credit cards, you won't even have them when you are tempted to run them up. This is not a bad idea, but if done too early can cost you lots of money and headaches.

Firstly, in the fine print of many credit card agreements, there is a paragraph that says what happens if you close your account with a balance. Unfortunately, what it often says is that your interest rate immediately jumps to the highest rate allowed by law for your particular area. This can add lots of interest costs to the process of clearing your debt. Many people realize this only too late and you cannot reopen the account once it is closed. I know this because I tried to do so and had to wait until I had repaired my credit to get another credit card.

Another reason that you may want to keep the account active, is because you may not get other offers for credit cards. Let's face it. If you are having trouble paying your bills as it is, you are in financial trouble. It is possible that you are going to miss bills and do damage to your credit. With damaged credit, you may have trouble getting credit in the future. This was certainly my experience. I closed all of my account and had bad credit. In order to repair my credit I needed a credit card (For some reason you need to have credit accounts like credit cards to qualify for necessary credit such as mortgages). However, with bad credit it was very difficult to get a credit card. Also, since you have already established a history with the companies you do business with, you have a longer credit history with them than with any companies you may deal with in the future. This long association is also positive to your credit. What is really best is to have a disciplined plan to pay down your debt, but keep your accounts open. You may need them in the future.

Of course, if you really want to, you can close all of your credit accounts. However, only do that once each account has been paid off. Never close credit accounts with a balance owing.

Communicate With Your Creditors

If your debts are current and you are having trouble paying them, sometimes the best thing you can do is to contact your creditors and try to reason with them. I know that sounds impossible but it is true and works sometimes. Large finance companies can be unsympathetic but other organizations like hospitals and private businesses can be more than willing to set up payment plans to help you out. This is true because they want their money and collecting on a very late bill can be expensive in both time and money. It is often more cost effective for them to set up a payment plan.

Setting Up A Payment Plan

Before you approach your creditor about setting up a payment plan, you should have an idea of what you want it to be like. Essentially, you need to do some planning. You need to decide how much you want to pay each month (make it reasonable but not burdensome), and when you can pay it. If you have a checking account, it might not be a bad idea to try and set up some sort of automatic checking account bill pay. Many banks offer this service free of charge and it will comfort your creditor.

Setting up a payment plan can be one of the best ways to clear a debt. If one of your creditors is happy to do this, TAKE THEM UP ON THE OFFER! This can completely eliminate a debt in a very controlled manner. Certain organizations like hospitals are often more than happy to set up payment plans. There are often income requirements to qualify for this. As a result, you may need to fax or mail you're your previous year tax return. This will allow the organization to verify you meet their qualification for setting up a payment plan.

Consumer Credit Advocates

With personal debt at an all time high, more people than ever before are experiencing trouble paying their bills. This is an unfortunate symptom of the epidemic levels of consumerism present in our society. As a result of this, a new type of non-profit and for-profit business model has developed. This model is that of the consumer credit advocate group.

In a nutshell, a consumer credit advocate will approach the creditors of their client and inform them that this person is in financial trouble. On behalf of their client, they try to persuade the creditors to set up more reasonable payment plans, lower interest rates and to waive fees to help with repayment. This type of assistance can be of enormous help. Many consumer credit advocates will also consolidate your bills. This is done by having you, the client, pay one sum to the credit advocate firm each month. Out of this all of your bills will be paid. This can alleviate the headache of keeping track of all of your bills and making sure that each one of them is paid on time. This also reassures your creditors, because they know that someone else that they can trust is handling the bill paying.

These services are not free. There is a monthly fee that you will have to pay to these firms in order to have them act on your behalf. These fees pay the salaries of the people that work for the firm as well as to expand the operations of the firm. These companies do perform a valuable service that is needed in increasing amounts these days.

All that being said, let me caution you. Before signing up with the services of a consumer credit advocacy firm, do your homework. Know that the firm is an upstanding member of the local business community. Contact your local Better Business Bureau (www.bbb.com) and see that they have a good reputation with the people that have dealt with them in the past. The Internet is another great place to check up on a company. Type their name into a search engine and see what comes up. You may be handing over your hard earned money to this firm at a time when you are in a weakened financial position; you need to KNOW that you can trust them.

You may be asking yourself why a creditor would agree to lower interest rates, wait longer for payment, waive fees, or establish payment plans. Well the simple answer is that it is good business to do so. If you do not pay your debt for one reason or another, eventually it will enter the collections process. In most cases, your debt will be sold to an independent collection agency at an enormous discount to the collection agent. In some cases discounts can go as high as 90%. That means that your creditor, in order to recoup some money, may sell your $1000 debt for as little as $100! It is a much better idea for a creditor to wait an extra 90 days without interest and collect the $1000 than to be forced to sell it for $100. This is why consumer credit advocacy groups can operate.

Debt Consolidation Loans

Another tool that you may want to consider, again if your bills are still current, is a debt consolidation loan. Now, these loans can be a problem if used improperly. You could, in theory, take out a debt consolidation loan, pay off all of your credit cards and then run them up again. At that time, you would have a debt consolidation loan to repay as well as being right back where you started with the credit cards. However, at that point, you would most likely not qualify for another loan. You could be in real trouble at that point.

Debt consolidation loans often use the equity you have stored in your house as collateral. Such loans are often called "Home Equity Debt Consolidation Loans". These can add even more dangers when you think that you are pledging the equity in your home to settle credit card debt. Failure to repay the loan could result in foreclosure.

As a general rule, I am not a fan of debt consolidation loans. I explored this option, but never acted on it. I decided that it would be best to pay off my accounts (the few that were current) on my own. I believe that this helped build my discipline an avoided the pitfall of another loan. Your situation might be different. You may already have taught yourself discipline and this option may be attractive to you. If it is, explore it and see what you find. My only word of caution is, once you pay off and consolidates your debts, don't generate new ones. Work hard to pay off the debt consolidation loan and move on to build your savings and investment portfolios.

If Your Debts Are **NOT** Current…

The techniques that we have discussed for paying off your debts in the preceding pages were all designed to address accounts that are current. If you are like I was, you will not have many of these. What we will talk about in the pages ahead are how to deal with accounts that are not current and most likely are in collections.

Accounts that are past due and are in collections are a different breed of animal than accounts that are current. These are the accounts that can rack up large interest charges and fees. These are also the types of accounts that can mar your credit record for years to come. However, there is a positive side. These accounts can often be paid off for much less than their face value and can ultimately save you a little money.

"Past Due" vs. "In Collections"

Before we really dive in, we need to establish some terminology so we are on the same page. That is, we need to clearly understand the difference between a "past due" account and an account "in collections".

A past due account is an account that is late. It can be any number of days late. What is important, however, is that this account still resides with the creditor who first issued the loan or credit.

For example, say you have not paid your credit card bill to ABC Bank in 60 days. This account is still with ABC Bank and has not been closed. This account is now 60 days past due. Because the account is still with the bank, there is a possibility that your delinquency has not been reported to a credit agency.

An account "in collections" is an account that has been sold to a collection agency. Essentially, what has happened is the initial creditor has given up any hope of receiving payment and has sold the debt to a second party. As I have said before, the collection agencies buy debts at deep discounts and hope they can get you to pay the full amount. That is how they make their money. Because the account is not with the initial creditor, there is a strong chance that this account would have been reported to a credit agency. In addition, instead of a delinquent account, this account will be reported as a "charge off" to the credit agencies. This is one of the worst marks that you can have on your credit report. This says that the creditor was forced to wait so long for payment that they gave up. This will bar you from a lot of credit account types in the future.

I always made accounts that were already in collections take a back seat to accounts that are past due. I figured if the account is already in collections and has been reported to a credit agency, and the damage was already done. I always focused my immediate efforts on paying the bills that were past due to prevent them from being closed and further tarnishing my credit history. A special type that always got top priority was an account placed with a collection agency that had not been reported to a credit agency. I took care of these right away as they were very close to damaging my credit but have not done so yet.

Essentially what I was doing here was a type of financial triage. I gave priority to accounts that I could save first. Only, when those accounts had been addressed did I move on to accounts that were in collections and accounts that had been reported to collection agencies. The way I figured it was that my bills were already past due and in collections, and I knew I already in trouble. I was going to have to pay finance charges, late fees and was going to suffer some damage to your credit. What I wanted to do was to limit these amounts and the damage as much as possible.

Dealing With Collection Agencies

If you are forced to deal with a collection agency, there are a few things that you should consider before you proceed.

Firstly, collection agencies are for profit companies. They are out to make money like the rest of us. That means that they will charge you fees and interest and want you to pay the full amount you owe. However, be aware, like I have said before, that these companies buy debts for pennies on the dollar. Knowing this fact can often give you the courage to make settlement offers you would otherwise be to shy to make or think are far too low.

Secondly, not all collection agencies are created equally. Some collection agencies are not to be trusted to honor their word. As such, you need to get EVERYTHING in writing. Any communication you make with a collection agency should be documented in some way. You should even write down the times and dates of phone calls to and from collection agencies. If you speak to an agent, ask for their name and identification number and record these as well.

Have them fax over a written offer spelling out all the points of any agreement that you agreed on. You will need a fax machine for this type of negotiation. Go to a local second hand store and I am sure you can find one for under $20. Ensure that it works before you start making any arrangements. Make sure that any settlement offers or payment plans are on company stationary with a logo and that it is signed. Unfortunately, a few bad apples will spoil the bunch, and unfortunately not all collection agencies will honor their word. The written information will be invaluable if they do not honor the agreement you made with them and you are forced to take them to court.

Lastly, you need to know that the behavior of collection agencies is strictly governed by law. Specifically, their actions and responsibilities are spelled out in the Fair Credit Reporting Act. This law is printed in its entirety in the appendix to this book. You should read through this act word for word and familiarize yourself with it. This law has been very helpful in my personal experience and I am sure that you can make use of it as well.

Setting Up Payment Plans

Many collection agencies will be willing to make payment plans with you. In many cases, they will be happy just to have someone pay some of the money that they are owed.

One thing that will be different is collection agencies will prefer a shorter payment plan. Something that is common is to pay half this month and half the next month. If this is something that is within your means and appeals to you, by all means explore this option. Before you run out and start making payment plan arrangements, you might want to read through the next section. What follows is another technique to eliminate your debt at a reduced rate.

Receiving and Offering Settlements

Many times in a last ditch effort to get payment before your account is sold to a collection agency; you will receive settlement offers from creditors. What these are, are offers to settle your debts for say 75% of their value. These are certainly worth considering and can save you a lot of money. Settling debts in this manner can spare you a lot of headaches too, especially if the account is only past due.

Collection agencies also will make settlement offers. Once my accounts were in collections for a while, they would send me all kinds of letters. Now, since these accounts had most likely been reported to a credit agency and have already damaged my credit, I looked at as "initial offers". Remember what I have said about collection agencies. They buy debt at very reduced prices and hope to make a profit by getting you to repay the full amount. That is all well and good; however, knowing this fact helped to save me a lot of money and trouble.

I also offered my own settlements to collection agencies. I thought of my communications with collection agencies as a negotiation game. They would make me an offer and I would make a counter offer. Back and forth we would go until we reached an arrangement you can both live with. They would still make their money, and I would eliminate a debt. Everyone was happy.

In order to make a settlement offer to a collection agency, make sure that you have the money that you are offering sitting in your account. If you cannot pay the bill, DO NOT MAKE THE OFFER! Wait until the last few days of the month. Another helpful fact about collection agencies is that they have quotas. They want to make sure they recover so many debts, worth so many dollars each month. Their representatives are under a lot of pressure to meet these goals. You can use this against them. Call them on the last day of the month and make your offer. The might be hesitant at first, make you a counter offer etc. Stick to your guns and get a number that you can live with. Remember, they are under pressure too. If the debt has been sent to the credit bureaus, get them to agree to remove this information as part of the settlement. If they believe you are serious about paying the debt and you throw out a reasonable dollar figure, they will most likely take it. **_Get it in writing!!!_**

Once you have the settlement offer, go ahead and pay the debt as agreed. Make sure that you fulfill you end of the agreement. If you pay by credit or debit card over the phone, ask for the "Authorization Number" and write it down. You also should ask for a "Clearance Letter". This is a letter again from the collection agency, saying, that the debt is paid and you have no further obligation to them. Have them fax this over once the payment has been made.

Put all of the documents relating to each of these transactions in a separate file and keep them somewhere safe. You may need them in the future to prove you have paid the debt.

Settlement Offer Document Checklist
- ✓ **Settlement Offer From Creditor**
- ✓ **Authorization Number or Receipt**
- ✓ **Clearance Letter**

Once you have paid the debt and have all of the documents listed above. You can consider the debt closed.

Declare Bankruptcy

I have never declared bankruptcy and the subject of bankruptcy law is a subject well beyond the scope of this book. In addition, recent changes in laws have made declaring bankruptcy much harder especially in the area of consumer debt.

Declaring bankruptcy should always be considered only as a last resort. Declaring bankruptcy will have long lasting and sometimes irreversible effects on your financial future and ability to rebuild.

If, however, you think that this is an option that will be good for your personal situation, and you see no other way out of financial difficulty, consult with a qualified and professional bankruptcy attorney.

Many people will simply go to the phone book to find an attorney. I have and I was very happy with the results. Personal referrals are another great way to find an attorney. If you know someone who has declared bankruptcy in the past, ask them about their experiences. Lastly, your state bar association is probably the best way to find a qualified attorney. Look for their website online. Most of these associations allow you to search through their members based on their location and areas of expertise. In these online database, you can find out a particular attorney's background, education, work experience and if there are any complaints about their service. Once you find an attorney you trust, be honest with them and follow their advice to the letter.

Conclusion

One time I was talking with a friend in a café. We were both in a similar situation financially, meaning we were both swimming in debt. We had both reached the point where we were actively trying to pay off our debts and we were both willing to discuss our mutual problems openly. He made the comment, jokingly, that he was very much looking forward to the time when he was worth nothing. I laughed and said I felt the same way. We parted ways, but for some reason, I have never forgotten those off the cuff words. They stuck with me. Eventually, over time as I struck away my debts, these words became a goal that I strove ever harder to reach. I kept telling myself with a smile that if I kept on working hard and was diligent, I would be worth nothing someday! One day, indeed, I was worth nothing. What a happy day that was!

This is a lesson that you should take to heart. Eliminating your debt should be your number one goal on the road to finding financial independence. Your debts may not be larger than your assets making you worth less than nothing like I was, but they still represent a financial burden that you need to eliminate. I did it and I have high hopes with hard work, you can do the same.

Chapter 5
Banks & Bank Accounts

In order to work towards your financial independence, you are going to need to save and invest your money. To do this, you will need to have a basic understanding of the banking and investment industries and the types of accounts that they offer. Think of this chapter as a very basic users guide for dealing with these institutions.

5.1 Financial Institution Basics

Very Brief Banking History

Banking started during the Italian Renaissance. At that point, Italian goldsmiths, who always had gold on hand, began to take deposits of other people's gold as well. They soon discovered that only a fraction of the people who had gold on deposit, would ask for their gold on any particular day. Knowing this, they realized that they could loan out the extra gold and earn interest from it. This had the result of increasing the money that was in circulation and creating more investment, jobs, and industry. Overall, society as a whole became more productive and this process eventually led to the modern world we live in today.

No matter what you might think of the banking industry today, or what experiences you have had with it, if you have money you need to put it somewhere. In most cases this will mean you need the services of a bank. You should be aware that there are several types of institutions that can serve as your bank. These are the commercial bank, the credit union, the online bank, the insurance company or the brokerage firm.

Commercial Banks

When most people think of a bank, they are thinking of a commercial bank. A commercial bank is owned either privately by a corporation or indirectly by shareholders who own stock in the bank.

Commercial banks are large banks that make their money through loans and fees. These banks often have very deep pockets and can finance anything from a used car to a new high rise office building. These banks frequently operate over large geographic areas such as several states or on a national or even global level.

Commercial banks are an excellent place to keep money that you need to have access to. They offer convenient access to your money at all hours of the night through their ATM networks. Commercial banks will offer any of the types of deposit accounts that will be discussed shortly. You can frequently find your same bank all over town and even in many cities across the country. Now, if you are like me, this access can create a problem. You may not be able to resist pulling some money out of your account any time you want. That is something to keep in mind when you decide how much money to keep in a commercial bank. Later in this chapter we will explore ways to make your money more inaccessible by utilizing the services of financial institutions other than banks.

These banks can afford to be selective with their customers. If you have bruised credit or have had problems with your bank accounts in the past, you may have trouble qualifying for an account at a commercial bank.

Credit Unions

Credit unions differ from commercial banks in several ways. Firstly, credit unions are member owned institutions. This frequently means that you need to join the credit union through an application process and you will need to maintain a minimum balance with the credit union. Minimum balances are frequently as lows as $5 dollars.

Another way that credit unions and commercial banks differ is there are membership requirements for joining a credit union. You may need to work at a particular business, belong to a union, or live in a particular area. Generally it is not difficult to find a credit union for which you qualify.

Credit unions offer most of the services that commercial banks offer, however, they generally operate on a smaller scale. It is not uncommon for a credit union to have only one or two branches in a single city. Credit unions will offer any of the types of deposit accounts covered in this chapter to individuals but frequently do not deal in business banking services. Credit unions offer their customers convenient access to their accounts through the ATMs owned by the credit union and often through a nationwide network of other credit unions all working together.

Credit unions are another option when deciding where you will keep your savings. They, like commercial banks, offer easy access to your money and this may be something you want to keep to a minimum.

Online Banks

With the introduction of the Internet, another type of bank has appeared. This is the Internet only bank. Now, we need to make a distinction before we proceed. There are commercial banks that offer their services online or in the branch and there are banks that have no branches at all. These types of banks operate over the Internet exclusively.

These banks offer the same deposit accounts that commercial banks and credit unions offer. They do not as a general rule own a network of ATMs, however. Generally, online banks will offer access to your money through a partnership with another financial institution that does maintain an ATM network. However, these can be difficult to find at times.

To deposit money to your account, you can transfer money from an existing bank account, or you can make a deposit through the mail with either a check or money order. This can take as long as a week in some cases.

These banks can be a little less convenient than a local commercial bank or credit union. However, this can be a blessing in disguise. Firstly, as a result of this, many online banks offer higher interest rates to convince customers to switch from a local bank. Secondly, this lag can often help to keep your money out of your hands when you get a wild spending urge.

Insurance Company Banking

Insurance companies are in the business of pooling risk. To do this, everyone pays into a large pot of money and, in the event of a disaster people make claims on the pot of money. However, statistically speaking, more people will pay more money into the pool than they will demand from it in compensation claims. The excess money is the profit for the insurance company.

With the easing of banking restrictions in the 1980s, a lot of insurance companies began to participate in the banking business. Why not? They had large sums of money lying around and they decided to begin lending it out in the form of loans. Eventually, these companies began to offer deposit accounts as well. When the Internet became very popular in the 1990s, many of these insurance companies started online banking operations.

Today, most major insurance companies will also offer "direct banking". This is the exact same service offered by exclusively online banks. You will have a deposit account and will be able to deposit money directly from an existing bank account. You can also mail in deposits. ATM access will be rather limited in most cases but you will most likely receive a debit card that can be used anywhere credit cards are accepted.

Due to the lack of ATM access and the fact that most insurance company banks will not have a location in your town, they are another good place to put money that you want to limit access to it. In addition, because of these fact, they often offer high interest rates to persuade you to keep your money in their institution.

Brokerage Firms

Brokerage firms also began to offer online banking operations in the late 1990s. It made sense. They were already trusted financial institutions and were completely established to transfer money electronically.

Today, these companies still offer deposit account service. Money, again, will need to be transferred from an existing account or mailed to the firm's secure post office box. You will receive an ATM/Debit card, but again ATM access may be limited. Like insurance companies and other online banks, brokerage firm banks will offer high rates of interest to make up for the lack of access.

In addition to standard deposit accounts, brokerage firms often offer what are called "sweep accounts". These accounts are not deposit accounts in the traditional sense. These are actually brokerage accounts that are intended to be used for the purchase of stocks and bonds. However, it is completely permitted to deposit money into these accounts and simply keep it there. There may be a quarterly fee if you do not make a certain number of trades every three months. These accounts often come with checks and ATM/Debit cards to allow for cash withdrawals. One thing to note with a brokerage account is that they are **not** FDIC insured and can lose value in the event of financial problems with the brokerage.

Brokerage firms also make a good place to keep money that you wish to save when you can't trust your own impulses.

FDIC

Before the Great Depression, anyone who deposited their money in a bank took a chance that the bank could go bankrupt and they would not be able to retrieve their money. This was a real concern and many banks did default during the Great Depression costing depositors enormous amounts of money. This created panic and further economic crisis. This effect only further increased the severity and length of the Great Depression.

When this happened the federal government realized that people who deposited their money in a bank, needed to feel certain they would be able to get their money back. Without this security, no one would deposit their money, banks had no money to loan, and no one could start a business to create jobs to end the Depression. As a result, the federal government created the Federal Deposit Insurance Corporation or FDIC in 1933. This corporation, backed by "the full faith and credit" of the United States government, ensured that depositors would receive their money in the event of a bank failure. It worked and people began to deposit money again. Eventually this helped end the Great Depression in this country.

Today the FDIC guarantees deposits of certain account types up to $100,000 *per depositor, per bank*. That last bit is important. If you have two accounts at one bank, valued together at $150,000, you are only insured up to $100,000. However, if you have $200,000 evenly split between two different banks, you are insured for the full $200,000.

The types of accounts that are covered are:

- Checking accounts
- Savings account
- Certificates of deposit
- Money market deposit accounts (Do not confuse these with money market funds.)

The FDIC does not insure accounts containing:

- Stocks
- Bonds
- Mutual funds

- Safe deposit boxes

Today it is rare to find a bank that does not have FDIC coverage but it is possible. One particular example would be a foreign bank operating within the boundaries of the United States. If you choose to bank with a financial institution that does not have FDIC coverage, be aware your account may lose value in the event of a bank failure.

NCUA

Credit Unions, which are not commercial banks, are insured by a different but similar federal agency. This agency is known as the National Credit Union Administration, or NCUA.

Along with regulating and monitoring the charters of the 8000+ credit unions in the U.S., the NCUA insures the deposits held at these institutions. Similarly, to the FDIC, most accounts at credit unions are insured up to $100,000. There have been recent changes in law that allow coverage of up to $200,000 on specific retirement accounts held at credit unions.

SIPC

The Securities Investor Protection Corporation is a non-profit corporation that protects investors from the failure of a brokerage firm. This institution is different from the FDIC and NCUA.

Firstly, while the FDIC and NCUA are federal organizations, the SIPC is not. It is a federally mandated corporation that is made up of member brokerage firms. Each of these firms pay into a general fund of money that is used to compensate investors in the event they are harmed financially by a failure of one of the member brokerages.

The SIPC does not compensate investors for losses on stocks and bonds. They will only compensate you if you are harmed by the failure of the brokerage itself.

5.2 Deposit Account Basics

Deposit accounts are simply accounts where you keep your money or assets. Many of the accounts that are offered by financial institutions are deposit accounts. These include checking, savings, MMDAs, CDs, brokerage accounts, IRAs and Roth IRAs. We are going to go over the basics of all of these accounts in a very broad, general manner. Whenever you open any account, you are strongly encouraged to seek the advice of a financial planner and thoroughly understand all specifics and requirements of the account.

Checking Accounts

Checking accounts are considered demand deposit accounts. You place money in your account and can write checks on the account demanding your money. These accounts are designed to provide frequent and recurring access to the funds in the account.

In the United States, most checking accounts are provided with an ATM/Debit card. This is a card that can be used directly at the bank's ATM network to withdraw cash.

In addition, this card may be used to make direct purchases anywhere credit cards are accepted. Instead of creating a debt that you must pay at a later date, the funds are deducted directly from your account.

These accounts are designed for convenience and are used to pay bills in most cases. Because of the convenience offered by these accounts, the frequently offer the lowest rate of all deposit account types. This is not true in all cases. Recently, some online banks have begun to offer checking accounts with all the standard conveniences but much higher interest rates..

Savings Accounts

Savings accounts are another type of demand deposit account. These types of accounts generally do not offer the convenience of access that is offered by checking accounts.

Normally, a savings account only comes with an ATM card. This can be used to withdraw cash from any ATM owned by the bank. You cannot write check on this type of deposit account.

Savings accounts are designed primarily as a reserve account. A good idea is to keep all of the money that you are planning to use right away (with a little cushion) in a checking account. Then you can use a savings account to hold your reserves.

A significant difference between a checking account and a savings account is in the rate of interest that is offered. While checking accounts frequently offer less than .5%, a savings account can earn interest rates that are equal to the Federal Funds Rate. (The Federal Funds Rate is the legally fixed amount of interest that banks have to pay the Federal Reserve Bank to borrow money.) Current and past Federal Funds Rates can be found at the Federal Reserve website (http://www.federalreserve.gov/fomc/fundsrate.htm).

Money Market Deposit Accounts

Money market deposit accounts (MMDAs) are a blend of the characteristics of both savings and checking accounts. These accounts offer access to the money held in them through debit cards and checks. However, there are frequently restrictions on the amount of checks that can be written and high fees if this limit is exceeded.

The stated purpose of these accounts is to preserve the purchasing power of the money in them. As such, these accounts often pay a high interest rate when compared to a checking account.

These accounts often have minimum balance requirement that you must maintain as well as minimum deposits when opening the account. These minimums are usually between $1,000 and $1,500. These accounts are also insured by the FDIC.

Certificates Of Deposit

Certificates of deposit (CDs) are a fixed term deposit account type. Essentially, you pledge to keep your money in the bank for a certain amount of time. Usually the term lengths start at 6 months. Towards the end of the term you will be contacted by the bank that holds your CD. They will ask you what you would like to do with the money. You can choose to purchase another CD, have the money deposited into an account that you specify, or have a check mailed to you.

In exchange for "locking" your money up for a certain period of time, you receive a higher interest rate than other types of deposit accounts. The longer that you pledge to keep your money in the bank, the higher the rate of interest that you can expect.

Banks are very happy to open a CD for you. This is money that they are certain will be in their bank and they can loan out. Any commercial bank or credit union will offer a CD account.

There are restrictions with a CD. Obviously, because of your pledge, you cannot have the money whenever you want. In most cases you can withdraw your money early, but you will have to pay a penalty of some kind. Usually this entails waiving all of the interest your money has earned over the last three months.

If you have had trouble with bank accounts in the past and have had trouble opening one recently, try offering to open a checking account and a CD at once. This strategy can be successful.

Essentially it says to the bank that you are more trustworthy and are willing to make a commitment. Some bank managers will be receptive to this idea and others will not.

Brokerage Accounts

Brokerage accounts are a deposit account at a brokerage firm used to buy stocks, bonds and mutual funds. These accounts are not insured by the FDIC but are backed by the SIPC in most cases.

These accounts are not designed to provide easy and immediate access to your money. They are designed to hold money and allow it to grow for long periods of time. Most of these accounts are not offered with ATM/Debit cards, although they do provide a moderate interest rate. You can also obtain checks for these accounts at times as well, often provided you meet a minimum account balance requirement.

These accounts are best used for what they are intended for, although you can use these accounts to store your money. Be advised that most brokerage firms will charge a quarterly maintenance fee if you do not make a certain number of trades during that period, or if you do not maintain a minimum balance.

IRAs

Individual Retirement Accounts (IRAs) are a special type of deposit account designed to encourage retirement savings. Just about any financial institution can open an IRA for you. You deposit money into an IRA just like any other account, but there are a number of restrictions.

Firstly, you can only deposit a certain amount of money each tax year (i.e. April 16th 2006 through April 15th 2007). This amount is set by Congress and does change depending on the year and current legislation.

Secondly, all contributions to an IRA are made on a pre-tax basis. This can create significant tax savings and add extra money to your savings and investment means. An example will help explain this idea. Say you make $30,000 a year and you can legally contribute $5,000 to an IRA this year. You deposit the $5,000 in your IRA. When tax time comes around, you can legally pay taxes on only $26,000. The other $5,000 you earned that is in your IRA is not taxed. At a 15% tax rate, that means you save $750 in taxes!

Thirdly, contributions to an IRA, cannot be withdrawn until you reach 59.5 years of age without incurring a 10% penalty and paying all subsequent taxes as well.

Now, there is a catch to all this. You will pay taxes on the money eventually. When you reach 59.5 years of age and begin to withdraw money from your account, you will be taxed on those withdrawals. However, as a result of your tax savings you will have a great deal more money to invest until that time. There are lots of specifics on IRAs that are well beyond the scope of this book. If you wish to open one of these accounts, consult a qualified tax professional for the best advice.

Roth IRAs

Roth IRAs are another type of retirement account that you can open. Most financial institutions that will open an IRA will also open a Roth IRA for you.

Like IRAs, there are contribution limits and early withdrawal penalties. The big difference between an IRA and a Roth IRA are in the manner in which the money is contributed. Money contributed to an IRA is on a pre-tax basis. Money contributed to a Roth IRA is on a post tax basis. This means that the money you contribute to a Roth IRA has already been taxed. The kicker is that when you reach the age of retirement, you can withdraw the money tax free. You can also withdraw money tax free under certain circumstances to purchase your first home.

Again, the rules governing these accounts are specific and technical. Consult a qualified tax professional for the best advice.

Conclusion

It will be essential in your quest to become financially independent that you are comfortable with the banking industry and the variety of accounts that you will encounter. If you work hard and begin to save in invest you will be forced to use these account types. It would be a good idea at this point to begin thinking about where you will be planning on banking and what types of accounts you will need. It would also not be a bad idea at this to find out what accounts are offered by convenient banks in your area.

Chapter 6
Saving Your Money

Once you are free of debt, you can move on to the next step in building your financial future and finding financial independence. That step is saving money. You will need to save money for many reasons. You may hope to retire someday. If you do, you need to start putting away money now. If you want to buy a house, you will need to make a cash down payment. Saving now for a few years down the road is a great way to do that. Maybe you want to take a vacation without going into debt. Saving money each month is a great way to enjoy a few weeks off without having to pay a fortune in interest payments for years to come. Maybe, you are like I am and cannot sleep unless you know you have a good pile of money in the bank in the event of an emergency.

For whatever reason you have decided to start saving, this chapter is going to discuss the basics of savings and a number of techniques that I used to start saving money. These techniques are designed for someone who has poor money control habits and essentially needs to automate and even trick themselves into saving. These were of enormous help to me as I discovered them and they can be of use to you as well. Good luck.

6.1 A Brief Explanation Of Interest

When you put money in a bank, the bank does not keep that money in their vaults collecting dust. Instead, the bank, loans out your money and charges interest for its use. The bank will often pay you a certain amount of the interest, because after all, it is your money they are using to make their loans. Of course, they pay you less than they receive. This is one of the ways that banks make money.

Interest, is essentially a fee paid for the rent of money. If you are going to begin saving money, you should have a good working knowledge of interest. This section, will give you a brief but adequate lesson on the subject.

As I have already stated, interest is money that is paid for the temporary use of money. Essentially it is a rental fee. Interest is always calculated on the principal, that is the money on deposit or loaned. For example, if you put $10,000 in a bank, they will pay you interest on a principal of $10,000.

To calculate interest, you will need an interest rate. There are two kinds of these. The first is a fixed rate of interest. This rate is set for the life of the deposit or loan. Fixed rates are common on home loans and certificates of deposit. The other type of interest rate is a variable rate. This type of rate will fluctuate over time. It is generally pegged to a rate of interest set by the Federal Reserve Bank and will go up or down according to that national rate. You will often find variable rates of interest on mortgages or deposit accounts such as a savings account.

Interest is calculated in one of two ways. The first is simple interest. The second method for calculating interest is compound interest. We are going to look at both of these two methods.

Simple interest is just that- simple. Essentially, interest is only calculated on the principle of the loan, no matter how much interest is paid. An example will help make this clear.

You have $1,000 and you wish to buy a bond. You do. You know have a bond worth $1,000. Bonds will be explained in more detail in a later chapter. This bond pays interest at 5% simple interest per year. This means that each year you hold the bond you will receive a payment of $50. This $50 is the interest, or fee, for the use of your money. If you hold the bond for 10 years, you will receive $500, but you will never receive more than 5% of $1,000, or $50 a year in interest.

Compound interest is different. Compound interest is calculated on the original principal, plus interest payments that are added to it. This adding of interest payments to the principal is called compounding and gives the name to this type of interest method. Interest can be compounded annually, semiannually, quarterly, monthly, or even daily. The more times the interest compounds, the greater the next interest payment will be.

Let's take a look at that $1,000 bond again. This time, however, let's assume the same 5% annual interest but compound the interest annually. This means that each year, the interest is added to the principal and the 5% for the following year is calculated using this new value. The first year you will receive 5% of $1,000 or $50. However, the second year, you will receive 5% of $1,050, or $52.50. Diagram 6.2 shows a side by side comparison of the two bonds over the same ten year period.

Looking at the total interest payments for the simple interest, you will notice that they remain at a constant $50. However, if you look at the second column, you notice that the interest payments begin to increase.

At the end of the 10 year period, you will notice that the total interest paid for the compound interest is much more than that paid for the simple interest. In this example the interest from the compound interest is $128.86 or almost 26% more. Remember, whenever you deposit money and receive interest, try to get compounding interest. Whenever you have to pay interest, try to arrange the interest as simple interest.

Year	$1,000 5% Simple Interest Payments	$1,000 5% Compound Interest Payments
1	$50	$50
2	$50	$52.50
3	$50	$55.12
4	$50	$57.88
5	$50	$60.77
6	$50	$63.81
7	$50	$67.00
8	$50	$70.35
9	$50	$73.87
10	$50	$77.56
Total Interest Paid	$500	$628.86

Figure 6.1 Comparison of simple and compound interest.

6.2 The Tithe

Many members of the Mormon Church voluntarily contribute 10% of their incomes to the church. This money is used to support the church, maintain its facilities, and support the charitable and missionary efforts of the church around the world.

The system that the Mormon Church has in place is largely responsible for the financial security of that church and the community it serves. It is also a wonderful system to try and mimic in you private life as you begin to save money and build your financial reserves.

When I was first beginning to save money, I remembered hearing about the voluntary tithe from a Mormon friend years ago. I thought to myself that this was a perfect model to use to begin building my savings. I made a goal to save ten cents of every dollar that I earned.

Making a goal and meeting it are two very different skills. I soon found that only a rigid self discipline could make this happen. What I would do was take the money that I made each day (at the time I was employed as a waiter and a large part of my income was tips that I took home everyday) and buy a money order for ten percent of that. Then, each night, I would address an envelope and mail the money order to an inconvenient bank (inconvenient banks will be discussed shortly).

With the money inconveniently tucked away and safe from my spending habits, my savings habits began to improve. Also, nothing reinforces a behavior like reaching and exceeding your goal. Eventually, I stopped using the 10% rule and began to obsessively save as much money as I could. Until you reach that point where you have a rigid self discipline, the 10% rule is a great way to get started.

6.3 Save Ten Thousand Dollars

The title of this subsection may be intimidating. If you are like I was, your bank account may never even have broken $1,000 let alone gotten anywhere near $10,000. However, you need to save $10,000 to really begin to approach financial independence and move on to investing your money to grow.

Let's explore this idea and develop it. It is very important concept and a thorough understanding of it will help you work towards this goal.

In the last chapter we talked about building a rainy day fund. This is an emergency fund to deal with small unforeseen problems. With $10,000 in the bank, you will be able to deal with much larger problems. Actually, you will be able to deal with most problems that are not a total catastrophe. Think about it for a minute. If your car is wrecked or breaks down, you can pay cash for a new one that day. If you lose your job, you have an ample supply of money until you find a new one. You needn't worry about going to the doctor for minor medical problems even without insurance. In addition, it would be very difficult to come up short on any of your bills with that kind of money in the bank. With $10,000 you have a good deal of financial security.

You need to save the $10,000 in a cash account. Do not tie it up in the form of a certificate of deposit. Having this money readily available will ensure your access to it when you need it. If the money is tied up in an investment, you may be forced to cash out of that investment at a severe loss if you need the money in a hurry.

Another added bonus of saving $10,000 is it will provide you with a great opportunity to establish a habit of saving. This self discipline will be an invaluable consequence and a great asset in the future. Just think about it. When I had no money, $10,000 felt about as far away as the moon. However, by working hard and saving like crazy I was able to reach my goal. I will tell you that actually seeing that much money in my bank account when I had been tens of thousands of dollars in debt only shortly before felt as good as walking on the moon. If you work hard and do the same you will feel like anything is possible.

6.4 The Immediate Benefits Of Saving Money

It may sound funny, but saving money can save you a lot of money. Think about it. If you have a decent amount of money saved up, you can pay bills all at once. This will eliminate finance charges. Many creditors, such as insurance companies, will offer you discounts for paying all at once. This improves their business cash flow and lowers you bills all at the same time.

If you maintain a minimum balance in your savings account you can also avoid fees that can quickly add up. This can be another added bonus.

Savings can actually make you money. If you have $10,000 in a high yield savings account, you can earn as much as 5% a year in interest. That means that for simply having $10,000 in your account you can receive $500 in interest payments. This money can be left in your account to earn ever increasing interest (by taking advantage of compound interest) or can be used as part of an annual vacation fund.

In addition to saving and earning you money, saving money can provide you with peace of mind. If you are like I was, you have lost many a good night's sleep to worrying how you are going to meet your expenses and how many collection and overdraft letters you will get in the mail the next day. This can have dramatic effects on your life and well being. You may not be focused for work the next day. You may suffer from depression and anxiety when you are awake. You may have recurring nightmares. This is no way to live. I definitely began to worry much less about these problems as my savings accounts increased in value. The knowledge that your bills can be paid even in the event of small unforeseen problems can be tremendously reassuring. Of all the immediate benefits of saving money, this one is the one I value most.

6.5 Decide To Keep Money Out Of Reach

When I was younger, anytime I had a bag of candy, it would be gone by nightfall. I had trouble leaving it alone and I would just eat one more at a time until nothing was left. I treated my money the exact same way. Whenever I had any money in the bank, I would make a list of how to spend it and I would scratch of the items on that list. Rarely would I receive a paycheck and not already have a plan on how to spend the money and no intention of saving any. It was sad. I had absolutely no self control and that had a lot to do with my finances spiraling out of control in the first place.

You may be the same way that I was. You may lack the discipline that is needed to begin to build your savings. If you work hard at teaching yourself to leave your money alone, eventually this discipline may come naturally. Until that time, you might need to keep your money out of your own hands to protect it from your moments of weakness.

Do not think of the need to hide your money from yourself as a weakness. Think of this decision as a strength. Realizing your limits and protecting yourself from them is a very wise step.

To actually keep your money out of reach, there are several steps you can take. We touched on this subject in Chapter 3 but will go over and add to those ideas here.

Consider using the services of an online bank or a bank that is not geographically convenient to you. Do not request an ATM or debit card. If you need money, you can call and request a check. This will take several business days. If there is an emergency, you can always complete a wire transfer to your local bank. This can be done very quickly in an afternoon. For full details on wire transfers, speak to your bank.

Another place that is completely safe to keep your money but is somewhat inaccessible is a safe deposit box. These are lock boxes in the vault of your bank. Banks rent these out for a small annual fee that depends on the size of the box. Small boxes frequently cost less than $20. To access the box you will need to visit the particular branch where the box is located. You will fill out a small slip of paper and, with your key, will be granted access to the box. You deposit or remove money as needed. Now, a safe deposit box is really only appropriate for occasional access. If you show up to the box every day or so, they will think you are a drug dealer and you could have some explaining to do. However, if you absolutely do not trust yourself around your money and wish to make it as inaccessible as possible, this is an option to consider.

Never keep cash around you. As I mentioned already, I worked as a waiter for tips for a long time. This meant that I had a lot of cash around. With my poor self control, very few of these tips ever made it anywhere productive. What I eventually started doing was buying a money order each night, as I have mentioned, after work with my tips. This took the cash out of my hands and much more of it made it to places where it could work for me instead of being used to buy something silly

6.6 Keep Track Of Your Money

It is a good idea to keep track of your money. Doing this has several benefits. Tracking your money will let you know just how much you have. This will prevent any overdrafts in your bank account and eliminate overdraft fees. You will also develop your self discipline by tracking your money. Nothing will reinforce your savings habit more than setting goals and watching as you achieve them.

To actually track your money you can use several options. The easiest way to organize your finances is to use a pen and paper. To use this system, buy a three ring binder and a "2 column" columnar pad. Columnar pads are a type of paper used for accounting and can be found at most office supply stores.

For each account, set up a register like the one in Example 6.2. Your "2-column" columnar pad should be laid out in a similar manner. In Column A on the left will be a preprinted line number. These are used to help you keep track of where you are on the page as well as giving each transaction a unique identifier. The Column B should be used for the date.

A	B	C	D	E		F	
#	Date	Trans. Description	+/-	Trans.		Balance	
1	9/15/07	Deposit Paycheck	+	663.	79	863.	79
2	9/16/07	Electric Bill Chk. 53	-	102.	75	761.	04
3	9/16/07	Garbage Bill Chk. 54	-	38.	62	722.	42
4	9/16/07	Cable Bill Chk. 55	-	50.	00	672.	42

Example 6.2 A common accounting format you can use to track your money.

The largest column (Column C) should be the transaction description column. Here you need to record a brief description of what the transaction is all about. You do not need to write a novel, but make sure you can understand what you meant even several years from the date it is written.

After the transaction column, there will be a smaller nondescript column. I use Column D to enter whether the transaction is positive or negative. This way, I can quickly eliminate a large portion of the records on a page if I am searching for a particular transaction. This step comes in very handy.

The next columns are the money columns. These are columns E and F. Together these two give the pad type its name. Column E is used to record the dollar value of the transaction that is being recorded. The second column (Column F) is used to track the balance of the account. For example, transaction #2 is a deduction of $102.75 from an account balance of $863.79. This leaves us with a balance of $761.04. This shows that after transaction #2 is accounted for, the balance of the account is $761.04.

I like the pen and paper method. It is old fashioned and simple. However, some people like to use a personal finance software system. There are a great many of these available. To find one, simply go to any office supply store. This way you can compare the different titles and find one that suits your needs.

These programs are very robust and are loaded with features. They can access all of your online accounts and compile reports and analyses on your spending habits, net worth, and investment returns.

For the computer savvy, these programs can make things very easy and for that, they are worth considering. They are also far from expensive. Many of the leading programs can be purchased for under $25.

6.7 Coins Can Add Up

If you live in a state that has a sales tax, and most of us do, you will receive a lot of coins in your change. This can be a real bonus in your efforts to save money.

To take advantage of this, all you need to do is make a rule that you will not spend any coins, only bills. Get a jar, a water jug, or some other receptacle (I use a 6" PVC pipe cap) and just start dropping in your coins. You should make sure that you will be able to lift the jug when it is full. I have known people who saved their coins in a 5 gallon water jug. When it was full, it must have weighed 200+ pounds! Just try wheeling that into the bank!

Once your receptacle is full, it is time to cash in your coins. Avoid machines that will turn your coins into cash as these often charge a fee for the service. Your best option is to find a bank that will process your coins without having you roll them and without charging a fee. I like to count money as much as the next person, but counting out five gallons of coins is a real headache.

When you have found a bank that will process your coins without making you roll them, you should have a plan on how to save the money. Since your coins are money that you have already paid taxes on, you might want to put the money in a Roth IRA. Any profits from investments will never be taxed that way. That is just one idea. Avoid spending the money as it will defeat the purpose of this whole exercise.

6.8 Found Money

At times in your life, you will receive money that you had not expected to. This can be a great occurrence and you should not waste it. Take this money and add it to your savings or investments. Don't do something silly like go out and buy a new and expensive car. It will just be in the junkyard in 10 years. However, carefully shepherded, your money can stay with you and continue to earn you income for the rest of your life. Examples of found money include:

- Gifts

- Bonuses at work
- Profit sharing checks
- Tax returns
- Inheritances

Take advantage of these windfalls and work to set yourself up for financial independence.

6.9 Automatic Savings Plans

One of the hardest things about learning to save is to get in the habit of savings. This sounds simple but it can be a real hurdle. You might read these pages and be inspired to start saving your money, and you might keep that dedication for a while. Eventually, however, it will fade a little. Another possibility is that you might simply forget one month and not get back into the habit.

One way to deal with both of these problems is to set up an automatic savings plan. These programs are designed to eliminate all of the guess work from saving by automatically deducting money form your checking account on a set date each month. Once the money is deducted, it is deposited into a high yield savings account for you. Once you set how much you want taken out each month, the program will run as long as you let it.

You will want to pay attention to how much you plan to deduct each month. Set it at a reasonable level to start. You can always change it later through the bank's online interface.

Finding a bank that offers automatic savings plans is not difficult. Many online banks offer these programs and commercial banks are beginning to follow suit. It is in the bank's interests to encourage you to save as well. The more of your money in their bank, the more they can loan out and earn in interest payments.

Conclusion

If you every hope to retire and live out your golden years on a tropical beach, you need to plan to supply yourself with money into those years. Saving (and even pinching) your pennies through your life, is the best possible way to build a fund of money to supply yourself with that income. The techniques presented in this chapter are only tools to this goal. What really matters is your mindset. You must focus your efforts and convince yourself that you are working towards a goal. Keep in mind that you are working and saving now so you can relax and enjoy your life in the future.

Chapter 7
Investing Your Money

Saving your money is a great goal. Saving your money is essentially the act of keeping and not spending money that you have earned. In a savings account you can earn a nice rate of interest. You keep your money in a cash form and can access it whenever you wish. This is nice and simple and safe. However, there is something else you can do with your excess savings. You can invest this money.

7.1 Basics Of Investing

Investing is the act of buying an asset with your money with the hopes that that asset will increase in value. Investing is different from saving in that you are converting your cash into a different asset type. An example will help to clear this up.

Let's look at an example most people are familiar with – buying a home. For the purposes of this example, let's assume that you have been very diligent in saving your money and have a whopping $200,000 in the bank. You go out and buy a house for $200,000. You pay cash and there is no mortgage. You now have no cash (not very wise but we will ignore that part) and you own a house worth $200,000. You have converted your assets from cash to a house. You have invested your money in this house and now own zero dollars and one house.

You may notice things are a little different from savings. Your money is now "tied up" in a house. You can sell the house and get your money back, but this is not as simple as going to an ATM. This is a fundamental difference between investing and saving. At times, your money will not be conveniently accessible. Also, if you need to convert your asset back into cash quickly, you may lose money by doing so.

Let's look at our example again. Let's say you have ignored my advice on gambling. You have made a bet with a bookie on a football game and lost. You now owe the bookie $5,000. Well you have no money in the bank because you just bought the house. You decide that you need to sell the house to pay the debt. Home prices have fallen in your area, but are expected to go back up shortly. You can now only sell your house for $190,000! If you sell now, you will lose $10,000!

In the last chapter, we talked about setting a goal of saving $10,000. This money is to be used as your emergency fund to eliminate your dependence on credit in the event of a problem.

However, the money has another purpose. Once you have $10,000 saved, you can begin to invest and reduce the risk you will need to sell any of your assets at a loss to pay smaller expenses that may come up unexpectedly.

Investing your money can also produce growth in your money. This is the part that encourages so many people to invest their money for retirement and profit on your original investment.

Let's look at are example one more time. Say you managed to pay off the bookie without selling your house. That was a good thing. Home prices have increased dramatically in your area and you can now sell your home for $250,000! That would represent a $50,000 profit.

No matter how much money you have, you can find a type of investment that you can afford, that can increase your money.

7.2 Scope of This Chapter

Before diving in to topic of investments, I want to point out the limited scope of this chapter. Investing is a very broad subject with many different facets that could fill a library with books the size of this one. Nothing close to every aspect of investing will be covered. In fact, this chapter should only be considered a very basic outline of simple ideas concerning investing.

The main goal of this chapter is to give you an idea of where to start your, hopefully, long investing career. This chapter will also give you basic questions to ask yourself about individual investments and a good idea of what more you may want to study.

To learn more about investing, there are many resources at your disposal. First, consider your local public library. Any public library in America will have a well stocked section on investing for your education. Check out and study a number of these books.

Brokerage firms want to help you to become an investor too. If you are not an investor, you will not buy securities and you will not pay their commission fees. To help you, many of these companies offer basic investor primers on the websites. Take advantage of these. The information is usually very current and will walk you through the specifics of using a particular company's website and services as well.

7.3 Basic Investment Types

Investments can come in many different forms. You can buy diamonds or gold directly with your money and this would be an investment. You can invest in classic cars. Essentially, you can turn your money into just about anything with the hopes of it going up in value.

There may be many investments that you can take advantage of, but, when you first start investing; most people should consider only four types. These investment types are:

- Individual Stocks
- Individual Bonds
- Mutual Funds
- Specialized Mutual Funds

Individual Stocks

"Stocks" are investments that most people have heard of. Unfortunately, not all of these people understand exactly what a "stock" is. . "Stock" is a fancy name for the property of a company, be that money, machinery, or buildings. The phrase "owning stock" is drawn from the fact that, through the ownership of shares in a company (shares are explained in the next few paragraphs), you own a part of the stock of a particular company.

Most companies are not owned by a single individual. Some are, but most are not. Instead most companies are owned by something called shareholders. Shareholders own "shares" or pieces of the company in question.

An example might help. You and 9 of your friends decide to buy a pack of cookies. There are 10 cookies in a pack and each pack costs $10. Each of you puts up a $1 and when the cookies have been bought, each of you owns a cookie. Each of you owns 10% of the shares in the pack of cookies.

Companies are the same way. Say a team of geologists have found oil somewhere. These people would like very much to pump out the oil and become millionaires. However, they are going to need $10,000,000 to get things going. So what happens is they start a company.

At first, this company is worth nothing. It is essentially a couple of geologists who know where some oil is and who own 100% of the share of a company that has no money. To raise the $10,000,000 they will need to sell some of their shares to investors. Investors will buy the shares for a certain amount of money with the hopes that the company will make a profit and the value of the share they own will increase in the future and they can sell them at a profit.

Companies can offer their stock in several ways. Firstly, they can offer them privately. That is where you as a person make an arrangement with a company to buy stock. Usually this type of arrangement involves large amounts of money. Additionally, private investments of this type may not be open to anyone. Existing shareholders and company directors can block the purchase of shares by an individual.

Stocks can also be sold publicly. Most of the companies that you can name will fall into this category, although there are a few exceptions. This means that the shares of a company are traded on an "exchange". An "exchange" is a fancy word for a place where stocks are traded. Originally, this meant an actual place; however, with the advent of the Internet, this increasingly happens in cyberspace.

Stocks that are traded publicly can be bought by anyone. No one can block you from the purchase of the shares of a publicly traded company. Also, shares in publicly traded companies are usually less expensive than the purchase of shares in a private company. Shares of publicly traded can be found from $.01-$100,000.

You cannot just go out and buy publicly traded shares directly. You will need to use a broker to buy your shares. A broker is a company that is directly connected to an exchange and can buy and sell stocks on that exchange. When you decide to buy or sell a stock, you will give specific instructions to your broker. They will carry out your instructions and charge you a small fee ($8-$25) for the service.

Stocks are generally the preferred security type if you are seeking long term growth for your money. Over time stocks tend to increase in value and return a higher rate of return than bonds. However, stocks tend to fluctuate in value more than bonds. This type of volatility can intimidate some investors.

Bonds

Bonds are a way of owning a debt that is owed by a company or government body. Let's explore with another example.

Say that your state has decided to build a new highway. This highway will be a financial blessing to your state. However, it will cost $50,000,000 to build it. Most states do not have this kind of money lying around in a bank and yours is probably no different. As a result, your state will need to raise the money somehow. They will do so by issuing bonds. Each bond will be issued with a face value of $1,000 and the state will pay a 5% interest rate.

What all this means is that someone (this can be a company or a person) will give the state $1,000 and receive a piece of paper saying that the state owes them $1,000. This is the bond. Each year the $1,000 is not repaid the state will pay the person $50 in interest. In essence, the state is taking out 50,000 loans for $1,000 each at 5% interest.

There are two main types of bonds. These are bonds that are issued by government agencies and bonds issued by corporations. Government bonds are often viewed as safer than corporations. As a result of this feeling, corporate bonds often pay a higher rate of interest. This is to encourage people to take the higher risk of corporate bonds.

In addition to government and corporate bonds, bonds are also divided into long and short terms bonds. Short term bonds generally last under one year. Long term bonds are those that last more than one year and can last as long as 30 years. The longer a bond lasts, the higher the interest rate that is offered to compensate for your money being tied up longer.

Bonds are also bought and sold through brokerages. However, the fees on bonds are often a little hard to figure out as they are frequently not listed by brokerages. Bonds are frequently only sold in amounts of $10,000 or more. If this seems like a lot of money to you (it is a lot of money), you may be much more comfortable owning bonds through mutual funds.

Bonds generally pay interest on a monthly basis. This means that money will be paid into your brokerage account each month or you will be sent a check. Due to the monthly payments, bonds are generally preferred by investors who need immediate income. Retired people often prefer bonds because of this fact.

Loan Your Money TO Uncle Sam

One of the largest borrowers of money in the world is the United States Government. The national debt is so large that it grows by **BILLIONS** of dollars each day. To see the actual value of the US debt, visit the Bureau of Public Debt website at http://www.treasurydirect.gov/NP/BPDLogin?application=np .

As strange as it sounds, this can benefit you. To finance the huge national debt, the US Government has a constant need to borrow money. This means that the US Government is always issuing bonds. If you have money that you would like to invest, US Government bonds and T-bills (bonds that are repaid within one year or less) are a great security to consider.

Bonds and T-bill sales are conducted by the Bureau of Public Debt. This is an office in the Department of the Treasury. The Bureau of Public Debt maintains a website (www.treasurydirect.gov) where you can learn about investing in government bonds through detailed tutorials and articles. You can also purchase bonds and T-bills directly through the site with an attached checking account. This is a great website that I have used many times over the years.

When I first started investing my money instead of saving it in the bank, I started with US Savings Bonds and moved to 1 Year T-bills. This helped me to get used to the idea that invested money would not be immediately available. Also, this very mild form of risk got me comfortable to take bigger investment risks in the future on such securities as stocks and corporate bonds. At the very least, do some homework, and check out the website and learn what types of bonds are offered and how they might benefit you.

Mutual Funds

Owning individual stocks and bonds can be a time consuming process. You need to keep a close eye on the financial profiles of each company whose stock you hold. You also need to be aware of all the credit analysis and credit risks to each bond that you hold. You need to buy when the stock is low and sell when it is high.

For many of us, this type of hands on investing can require more time than we can spare. We have lives to live. We have family responsibilities and want to get away for vacations now and again. This is where mutual funds come into play.

Mutual funds are a collection of many investors' money that is directed by a professional money manager. Instead of buying the stocks and bonds held in the fund, you buy shares in the fund itself. With your invested money and the money of the other investors, the fund manager then buys securities (the types of securities are governed by the fund's goals and rules) with the plan to earn a return on the investment. When the fund realizes a profit, the value of the shares of the fund you hold will increase in value or the fund may pay out money in the form of a dividend (to be discussed shortly).

Mutual funds are nice because the investments are carefully monitored by professionals trained in the art and science of money management. You do not have to watch every day to look for trends emerging in the stock market. You do not have to be up to date on the sales statistics of each of the companies whose stock you hold. That is the job of the money manager.

Now there is a catch. The direction of the money manager is not free. There are fees associated with owning mutual funds. Each time the fund manager conducts a trade; there are brokerage commission costs that need to be paid. Also the manager and their staff have salaries that need to be paid as well. All of these costs are paid out of the profits on the investments before the money is passed on to the shareholders. Pay close attention to these fees. Some of them are reasonable and others are not. Before investing in a mutual fund, compare the fee structure to similar funds and see how they stack up.

Mutual funds are generally bought directly from the investment company that manages the fund. You wish to look for so called "no load" funds. This means that there is no cost to buy the shares of the fund. The investment company will make its money from the fees of managing your money in the fund and not from commissions at the beginning. There are usually minimum investment amounts for mutual funds. These can range depending on the company and the type of account you wish to open. If you wish to open an IRA with the investment company, minimum initial investments can be as low as $1,000. If you wish to open a general investment account that you can withdraw funds from at your pleasure, the minimums generally range from $2,500 to $5,000.

Specialized Mutual Funds

Mutual funds can place your money in just about any type of investment you can think of. You need to understand these different types of funds and know how you can use them in your financial planning.

Stock Funds

Stock funds as their name implies are mutual funds that invest only in stocks. They can buy the stocks of any type of company but most will target stocks of a specific type. These types are:

- Small Cap Stocks
- Mid Cap Stocks
- Large Cap Stocks
- Value Stocks
- Growth Stocks
- Foreign Stocks

Small cap stocks are the stocks of companies whose total assets are worth less than $1 billion dollars. These are newer companies that may have just issued public stock for the first time or who do not have long histories. These companies also may be smaller niche companies with proven business models of limited scope. These companies tend to offer new and innovative products and services that are growing in popularity. Small cap companies tend to offer a higher risk than large cap companies simply from the fact that they have less money and assets at their disposal in the event of financial troubles or a recession. However, the new products and services offered by these companies can make them some of the most profitable stocks to invest in.

Mid cap stocks are the stocks of companies with a total value of between $1 billion and $10 billion. These companies are often industry leaders in a particular business sector. They are well established and often have operations in many countries. Mid cap companies were small cap companies not long ago in most cases. These companies are often dominant in a specific market or a specific country. Many technology firms that exist today are mid cap companies. These companies tend to have more durability because of their higher value than smaller companies; however, they often are industry leaders in development and research. As a result of this combination, mid cap companies offer higher profit opportunities with a lower risk than small cap companies.

Lastly there are the large cap companies. These are companies with a total value of more than $10 billion dollars. Large cap companies frequently have operations in almost every country on earth. These companies have wide and extensive business dealings and they tend to dominate a particular industry or industries. These companies often have long histories of business going back more than 100 years in some cases. Large cap companies, in most cases, are not going anywhere anytime soon. They have deep financial and credit reserves that allow them to survive even the most trying financial environment. These companies frequently make products with household names with which you are familiar. These companies often have much lower risks than younger, smaller companies. However, as a whole this size company will provide fewer profit opportunities than the younger, smaller companies as well.

Value stocks, are the stocks of companies that have a long history of successful operation. These are companies that have a large value in their underlying assets and proven sales of products or services. These are companies that will continue in successful operation even during economic troubles. Take for example a well known drug brand. Let's face it; even if you are unemployed, you are still going to buy your heart medication. This is the reason that many drug companies are a typical example of a value stock. Most companies that fall into the class of large cap stocks are considered value stocks.

Growth stocks are the stocks of newer companies that have a great potential to become a big very profitable company. Say a new biotech company composed of only a few patent holding doctors has developed a revolutionary artificial heart. This is a new small company but the technology that this company offers could quickly make it a major force in the biotech industry. This type of company is considered a growth stock company. Most small and mid cap stocks are considered growth stocks.

Foreign stock funds invest in companies that are not based in the United States. These funds can invest in a particular area (i.e. Europe), country (i.e. Sweden), or economic class (i.e. developing countries). Foreign stocks can be broken down into all the preceding categories as well. Foreign stocks can help balance risk in your portfolio. While one geographic area is doing poorly, another may be doing well.

Bond Funds

Just like stocks, bond investing requires time and effort to protect your money. Again, not many of us have the time that is required. Bond funds are the answer these people are seeking. Bonds funds allow people to invest in bonds and receive immediate income without the need to carefully monitor the credit risk and status of each government or corporation or country whose bonds you hold.

Another reason to invest in bond funds is to manage your risk that a bond issuer may not repay the money. If you have $10,000 in bonds with one particular government and that government defaults on its debt, you will lose most if not all of your investment. However, if you have $10,000 invested in a bond fund that holds bonds from 300 corporations and governments and one of these corporation defaults, you will lose only a small portion of your investment.

Bond funds occur in several different flavors. These include:

- Short Term
- Intermediate Term
- Long Term
- Government
- Municipal
- Corporate
- Foreign

Short term bond funds only invest in short term bonds. These are bonds that are generally under one year in length. The rates of interest returned by these funds in generally lower than longer term bond funds. However, these funds do not suffer from interest rate risks that can seriously lower the fund share price of longer term funds.

Intermediate term bond funds invest in bonds whose terms range in length from 1 to 10 years. These funds offer higher rates of interest than short term funds. This higher rate of return is offset by an increased risk from interest rate increases.

Long term bond funds hold bonds from 10 to 30 years in length. These funds return an even higher rate of interest than intermediate funds. These funds are especially sensitive to interest rate risks.

Many bond funds only invest in government bonds. These funds frequently will hold short, intermediate and long term bonds but only of government issue. The appeal of funds of this type is that governments (at least inside the United States) almost always pay their debt. This makes them a fairly reliable source of income.

A special type of government bonds are known as municipal bonds or "munis" for short. In the United States a municipal bond is a bond issued by other than the Federal Government. This means a state, county or even city. The risk of default by these governments is slightly higher than with the Federal Government but less than a corporate bond.

Corporate bond funds only invest in corporate bonds. These are bonds issued by large corporations when they need to raise billions of dollars for new power plants, cable networks, or automotive factories. These bonds often pay higher rates of interest than government bonds. The reason for this is that at times U.S. corporations do fail to pay their debts and you run that risk when investing in corporate bonds.

The last major type of bond fund that I will discuss is foreign bond funds. These are funds that buy the bonds of foreign governments and corporations. In addition to all of the risks so far discussed, these funds suffer from political risks. It is not impossible that the countries where some of these bonds originate may suffer economic crises, coups, or even wars. This can cause defaults and loss of investment. However, your fund manager is aware of this and will do their best to protect you from this risk by holding bonds from many different entities and buying and selling bonds as events unfold. The attraction of foreign bond funds is that they often return rates of interest even higher than domestic corporate bonds.

7.4 Exchange Traded Funds

Normally, to invest in a mutual fund, you open an account with the company that offers the fund and send them money. There are often minimum investment amounts of between $1,000 and $5,000.

There is, however, an alternative. There are mutual funds known as "Exchange Traded Funds" or ETFs. These mutual funds are bought and sold just like stocks. The beautiful part about ETFs is you can invest in as little as one share of a mutual fund. A single share of an ETF can be bought for as little as a few dollars.

To buy an ETF, you will need a brokerage account just like when you buy a stock. There will be commission charges for each purchase or sale you conduct. Again, these range from $8-$30, depending on the brokerage firm. Now, obviously, it would be silly to pay an $8 commission to buy a $7 ETF. However, if you want to invest a $500 Christmas bonus check in a mutual fund, you can easily do so with $500 of ETF shares and avoid the headache of investment accounts.

7.5 Index Funds

There is one last mutual fund type that I want to talk about. This is the index fund.

Indexes are basically a group of stocks that have some similarity such as being in the same industry, same geographic area or valuation (such as small, mid, and large cap companies). During the course of the year, some of these companies will increase in value and others will decrease in value. There is no way to know which companies will increase or decrease.

To take advantage of this situation, there is an approach to investing called index investing. This means buying ALL of the stocks in the index. The stock will also be bought in a ratio that represents their "weight" in the index.

For example, imagine a company called ABC Mining. ABC Mining is one of the fifty companies that make up the Mining Index. All of the companies in the Mining Index have a total value of $100 billion dollars. ABC Mining is worth 2.5 Billion or 2.5% of the mining index. Using the technique of index investing to invest in the Mining Index, you will invest 2.5% of your money in ABC mining. If you have $10,000 to invest, you will invest $250 in ABC mining.

As companies grow and shrink, their weights in the index will change and you will need to adjust their weight in your portfolio as well. This can be time consuming. That is what index funds will do for you. Again, there is a manager, and their job is only to keep everything weighted appropriately. Also companies will drop out of the index and be added to the index. Manager will make these adjustments as well. The managers just mimic what the index does. Index fund managers do not make decisions based on their beliefs. This is called passive management.

There are two good things about index funds. Firstly, the fees are generally lower. While a fund that is actively managed may charge 5% a year, a passively managed fund generally charges less than 1%. Over 40 years of investing, this can really add to your portfolios bottom line. Another benefit of index funds is they tend to return better results than actively managed funds <u>over long periods</u>. This is not a guarantee that you will make money, but the odds are in your favor over long periods. If you are considering investing in mutual funds, do some deep research into index funds and give these funds some serious thought.

7.6 REITs

Real estate has been a very popular and lucrative investment type for the last several years. If you are like me, you are tired of hearing about all the money your friends made in the real estate market over the last few years. Many people think that the only way to invest in real estate is to directly own a piece of property. This is simply not true.

There are mutual funds that invest solely in real estate. These funds are referred to by the name Real Estate Investment Trusts (REITs). In a nutshell, these funds amass billions of dollars and then buy and sell, or rent, large pieces of real estate such as malls, office parks, storage facilities, and apartment complexes. These funds make money through the receipt of rent payments or the sale of investment properties at higher prices than were paid.

In most cases, each month, if you hold shares of these funds, you will receive a monthly rent check. Wouldn't it feel nice to receive a rent check instead of writing one for a change?

7.7 Options, Futures, Commodities and Currency Trading

The investment types that we have talked about so far are pretty basic in nature. You either buy a stock, a bond, or a mutual fund that holds these types of securities. Maybe you want to dabble with REITs. This is by no means an exhaustive list of investment strategies or securities. These are simply the types of investments that beginners should start with.

If you begin to invest and build a portfolio, you will no doubt begin to hear about another four types of investing. These are:

- Options Contracts- Contracts that allow you to buy or sell a security in the event a certain price occurs. These differ from futures in that you have the *option* to buy or sell the security.
- Futures Contracts- Contracts that oblige someone to buy or sell a particular security at a specific time at a specific price. Futures mean that you *must* buy or sell the security.
- Commodities investing – is the buying and selling of certain natural products such as gold, oil or wheat. This is frequently carried out with a futures contract.
- Currency trading – is the buying and selling of foreign currency with the hope that it will increase in value.

These four types of investing could be called "advanced" investing. These are not a good place to start. Investing in these types of securities and strategies can involve serious risk to your money. In some situations, you can even lose more money than you originally invested.

7.8 Finding A Brokerage

Finding a broker is an extremely important task. You need to have confidence in a stock broker the same way that you have confidence in your bank. After all, it is entirely possible your broker will have as much more of your money that your bank.

There are many national brands that advertise on every type of media out there. You probably know a few names already. These can be a good place to start. They have a well known pedigree and large financial resources behind them. Pick a few and ask them for a new investor kit. These will offer many specifics about that particular brokerage.

If you have never heard of any stock brokerage, try typing in "choosing a stock broker" onto any Internet search engine. This will bring up a long list of relatively current articles that will discuss the merits and drawbacks of many well known respectable brokerage houses. Read quite a few of these. They will help you make an educated decision.

7.9 Returns on Investment

The whole point of investing is to increase your money. There are four ways this can be done that we are going to talk about. The first means is by receiving dividends, the second way is through capital gains. Lastly, you can receive interest payments from bonds. We are going to explore each in turn.

Dividends are cash payments made to shareholders. It's that simple. Dividends can be issued regularly, on a monthly, quarterly, or annual basis. They can also be offered during times of great profit, when the company wishes to distribute its profits directly to its shareholders instead of reinvesting them.

Many companies that have stocks, whose prices fluctuate a good deal, will offer high dividends. This is a way to make the stock more attractive to investors. These amounts can fluctuate over time.

Capital gains are another way that you earn a return on your investment. This is the old "buy low, sell high" approach. Let's look at an example to illustrate this point. You buy 10 shares of ABC Mining for $10 each, or a total of $100. After one year, each share of ABC Mining is worth $11 each, or a total of $110. This means that you investment is worth $10 or 10% more than when you bought it. However, this is not money yet. ABC Mining may have a mine accident that causes its stock price to fall and this potential return to disappear. To realize the gain in your capital (your money) you would need to sell ABC Mining while its shares are worth $11.

If you hold bonds or bond funds of any kind you will receive interest payments. These will be paid to you on a regular basis at a fixed rate. If you invest in a bond fund, you will receive a small payment for each share of the fund that you own. If you own bonds directly, it is most likely that interest payments will be made to your investment account.

Lastly, if you own a REIT of any kind you will receive rent payments. These are disbursed just like bond interest payments and stock dividends. For each share of the trust that you own, you will receive a small rent payment. These too will be deposited to your investment account on a monthly basis.

7.10 Understanding Your Investment & Risk

Investing is different from savings in another very important way. While locking your money in the bank guarantees its safety, investing can put it at risk. At times, this risk is minimal. At times, your risk can be very significant. To protect your money, it is essential that you understand the risk to each of your investments.

One of the best ways to understand the risk to your investments is to read something called a prospectus. A prospectus is a publication that is made available to investors. In the case of a stock, the company that issued the stock will make it available. In the case of a bond or mutual fund, the investment house that oversees that security (security is a fancy word for investment) will issue the prospectus. Prospectuses are frequently updated and if you are a current investor you will automatically be mailed a current copy each time it changes.

Inside a prospectus, you will find a section specifically addressing any potential risks to the investment. Read these. Understand these. If you do not understand the section on risk, find someone who does and seek their counsel. This can be a parent, friend, or financial planner, however, make sure you trust them. Do not seek the advice of someone who is paid a commission for selling you investments. Their advice is not objective and should be viewed with caution.

In addition to risk, you will find many other useful bits of information. These should be read and understood as well. The first of these bits of information, in the event of a mutual fund, is the objective of the fund. This will tell you the goal of the fund. Essentially, what the management company hopes to achieve with your money.

Understanding just what you are investing in is very important as well. It would be foolish to buy a stock and have no idea what the company does. To learn about the operations of a company whose stock you own, another document called the annual report is essential. This document, as its name implies, is published each year. Usually, you will need to find the previous year's report. This can be done on the company's website in most cases. If not, you can find an investor relations department phone number and they will mail you a copy.

Inside an annual report you will find a wealth of information. This information includes:

- Current Operations
- Profits & Losses
- Financial Holdings and Debts
- Future Risk Analysis

If you are going to invest in a company it is not unwise to obtain a copy of their annual report and read it cover to cover. After all, wouldn't you prefer spending some time reading than replacing the $5,000 you lost because you did not understand your investment?

Conclusion

Hopefully, you have learned something about investing your money in this chapter. Now it is up to you. Go out and start doing your homework. Check out some of the websites listed in this chapter. See what they have to offer and if it appeals to you. Start reading the business section of your paper or some of the many financial publications on the website.

Most importantly decide which type of investment strategy you like the most. Then, go to the library or the bookstore and get some books on the subject. Then, read them. If you haven't saved up $10,000 and are working towards that goal, consider this period time to prepare. Once you have saved $10,000, you can begin to invest your daily or weekly tithe instead of saving it. If you already have the knowledge and don't need to waste time doing so, you will be ahead of the game. In investing, being ahead of the game means more money.

Chapter 8
Insurance: Protecting What You Have

One of the sad facts of life is that things do not always go as planned. This is where insurance comes in. Insurance provides you with financial assistance in the event that misfortune should strike. Insurance is not a subject to be taken lightly. If you have insurance that you do not need, you are wasting money that could be invested elsewhere. If you do not have enough coverage, you could be putting yourself, your family and your finances in grave danger.

As with the chapter on investing, this chapter is by no means an exhaustive discussion on the subject of insurance coverage. You are strongly advised to seek the counsel of professionals in making decisions of this magnitude. They alone have the thorough knowledge and background to give you sound advice. The types of insurance presented here are merely a collection of insurance policies that are thought to be of interest to the readers of this book and are intended to give you a basic place to start further research.

8.1 Auto Insurance

Auto insurance is unique where insurance is concerned in that you are legally required to carry a policy if you drive a car. More specifically, you must carry a liability policy.

Liability insurance is required less for your protection and more for the protection of people that you may injure or whose property you may damage. As a general rule, you receive no protection from injury or property damage for yourself if you only carry liability insurance. For instance, if you were at fault in an auto accident where your car was a total loss, with only liability coverage you would need to replace your car yourself. The insurance company would not assist you with that matter.

Coverage for liability insurance is divided into two categories. The first is called "per accident" and the second is "per person". Per accident coverage is the total amount of money that the insurance company will pay for damages arising from a single accident. Assume, for example, you are driving a vehicle that crashes into a building worth $200,000. If you only carry $100,000 in per accident coverage, the insurance company will only cover damages up to $100,000. You will be responsible for the other $100,000.

Per person coverage deals more with medical injuries that may arise from an accident. If you carry $100,000 in per person damage coverage, and you injure four people in a car accident, each of these persons will be eligible to claim up to $100,000 in damages (a total of $400,000) from your insurance company.

There is a debate concerning what amounts of "per person" and "per accident" coverage you should carry. As I have said before, I am not a professional and do not seek to offer professional advice. As such, you are best served by talking with friends, family and professionals who can offer you more personal and relevant advice in determining a proper amount of coverage.

Beyond simple liability coverage, there are a number of auto insurance policy additions you can add for your personal protection as well. We will discuss:

- Comprehensive Auto Insurance
- Supplemental Medical Coverage
- Uninsured Driver Insurance

Comprehensive insurance will protect <u>you</u> from property loss arising from an accident. Essentially, this will replace your vehicle to pre-loss condition in the event of an accident. Any time that you have an auto loan for the vehicle you are driving, you will be obliged to carry comprehensive insurance. If you own your car outright, this coverage is optional. If you can afford to replace your car, this coverage may be unnecessary. Discuss this option with your insurance agent.

It will not matter whether you are at fault or not in the accident, the insurance company will replace your car. However, your future insurance rates may increase as a result of a claim of this type. Generally with a comprehensive policy, you will have a cost known as a deductible. This is the amount that you will contribute to repairing your car. For example, if you have a $500 deductible and there is $1,000 in damage to your vehicle, the insurance company will cover the $500 above your deductible. Generally speaking, the higher your deductible is, the less your comprehensive insurance will cost.

You may be hurt in an auto accident and you may have medical bills because of this. Medical bills can be some of the biggest arising from an accident. To protect yourself from this you can add additional medical coverage to your auto policy. This type of medical coverage will only protect you from medical costs stemming from a car accident. You cannot use it if you need a flu shot. This type of coverage would be a good idea if you have no medical coverage at all or you believe that you need to supplement your existing medical coverage.

Uninsured motorist coverage will protect you from costs associated with repairing your person and vehicle from an accident, where, you were not at fault but the other driver was uninsured. Sadly, these people do exist and this coverage is not a waste at time to consider.

8.2 Renter's Insurance

If you rent your home, you should not be without renter's insurance. Renter's insurance, in a nutshell, protects all of your property inside your rented space whether it is a house or apartment.

Many people labor under the incorrect assumption that in the event of a disaster such as a fire, the insurance policy of the landlord will replace their items. This is not the case. Your landlord most likely does have an insurance policy for your rented property, but that will only cover the loss of the building itself. That check will go to the landlord, not you.

How many of us could afford to replace everything that we own in the event of a disaster like a fire? Most of us could not afford to. That is why you need to consider renter's insurance. In addition to protecting your assets, renter's insurance protects you from liability claims arising from your rented property. This means that is a pizza delivery man slips on your porch and sues you, the insurance company will be there to assist you with legal costs and compensation during the lawsuit

Finding renter's insurance is not hard. Any major insurance company or insurance agent will be able to write a policy for you. Again, make sure that you buy enough coverage to replace your items, but not too much that you are wasting your money on insurance premiums.

The costs of renter's insurance are generally very low and are far outweighed by the risks that these policies manage. Your costs will vary considerably from region to region and depending on the specifics of your location. You can obtain quotes from many online insurance companies simply by using the Internet.

8.3 Homeowner's Insurance

Homeowner's insurance will offer all of the protection that renter's insurance offers, however, it will also protect you against the loss of the home itself. If you have a mortgage (most of us will), you will be required to carry homeowner's insurance. This protects the lender in the event that your house is destroyed. Essentially it guarantees that they will be repaid even if the house is a total loss. Often, you can have this cost rolled into your monthly mortgage payment. Shop around and compare costs before you accept any offers.

One thing worth noting is that homeowner's insurance does not cover floods. Floods can strike anywhere. Floods do not only occur in areas close to rivers. The Federal Government, through the National Flood Insurance Program, helps to make flood insurance available. To find out more about this program, visit their website at www.floodsmart.gov.

8.4 Disability Income Insurance

Disability income insurance is a less known but highly desirable insurance policy type. This policy will provide you with income in the event that you are injured and not able to return to work.

Many of us will be familiar with worker's compensation insurance or "worker's comp". Worker's comp insurance will cover your medical costs, rehabilitation, and expenses in the event you are injured or disabled *at work*. However, if you are injured or disabled when your car slides of the road on your way to work, you will have no protection.

Stop and consider that for a second. You are injured in a car accident in which your car is the only one involved. There is no insurance company you can sue for damages. Your legs are badly injured requiring one year of rehabilitation. If you have medical insurance, your recovery and rehab will be covered. However, your living costs will not be covered. How do you pay your mortgage, electricity or food bills while you cannot work? You may have savings, but how many of us can live a full year without any income?

This is where disability income insurance comes in to play. Some statistics say you have a one in six chance of being disabled at one point in your life. In the event that this situation does occur, disability income insurance will help provide you with money to cover day to day expenses while you recover and protect you from bankruptcy.

The costs of disability income insurance vary widely. It depends in large part on your profession. If you are in a high risk field with physical demands such as construction, you will be a higher risk and need to pay a higher price for coverage. Also the amount of monthly income you wish to receive in the event you are injured will help to determine your costs. If you want to receive $1,000 a month while you are injured, you will pay one premium amount. If you want to receive $5,000 a month when you are injured, you will obviously pay a higher premium.

The amount of income you can receive in the event that you are injured is governed by law. This amount does change with time but is given by a percentage of your previous year's income as reported by you to the Internal Revenue Service. Your insurance agent will be able to inform you of the amount of income you can receive.

Another important consideration when shopping for a disability income policy is known as the "elimination period". The elimination period is the amount of time that you must to wait before you can receive income from the insurance company in the event you are disabled and cannot work. During this period, you will be dependent on your savings to provide yourself with financial support.

The purpose of the elimination period is to reduce the times when you will need to make claims on your policy. If you sprain your ankle and cannot work for 10 days and have a 60 day elimination period, you obviously cannot make a claim. Similarly to deductibles, the longer the elimination period, the lower your premiums will be. Sixty to ninety day elimination periods are common.

8.5 Life Insurance

Life insurance is a policy type that provides your family with money to cover costs in the event of your death. There are two types of life insurance. These are term and whole life insurance.

Term life insurance is coverage that you purchase that lasts a specific amount of time or "term". Examples are very helpful in explaining life insurance. Let's say you and your husband buy a home. You now have a shared debt to the mortgage company. You use both of your incomes to pay the mortgage bill each month. However, in the event of one of your deaths, neither of you could afford to pay the mortgage alone. This would result in forcing the survivor to sell the home or risk going into foreclosure. Now, your mortgage only lasts for 30 years and then the house will be paid off. To manage this risk you can buy a term life insurance policy that lasts for 30 years and will provide any survivor with enough money to pay off the house. Use term life insurance to protect yourself from risks that last a set amount of time.

Whole life insurance lasts your whole life. Essentially, this type of insurance will provide money to cover your funeral costs when you die. This type of insurance is much cheaper to purchase when you are young. Any insurance agent will be happy to discuss this type of policy with you.

8.6 Medical Insurance

No other insurance type is as important as medical insurance. We all get sick from time to time and the costs of a serious medical problem can burden if not bankrupt most people. A hospital stay lasting three nights can easily cost $25,000. To protect yourself you need to carry medical insurance. Buying medical insurance can be very costly but the risks are simply too great to ignore.

As with auto insurance, medical insurance policies have a deductible. This is the amount above which the insurance company will cover the bills for qualified expenses. When bills are below this amount, you will often need to pay them. The higher the deductible, the lower the costs of the monthly premiums will be.

Businesses that employ a certain number of employees are required to offer a group medical insurance plan. This can be a great benefit if you are an employee of one of these companies. Just like wholesale retail stores, when you buy a large number of policies at once, you can command a lower price. This means that the costs of the plans are lower to begin with. In addition to lower costs from the beginning, workplace medical insurance policies are often subsidized by the employer. Essentially what this means is that the employer has an interest in making sure that their employees are healthy. Fewer missed days of work can mean more profits for the company. To encourage the health of the employees the employer will pay a part of the costs of the medical insurance plan. This means that the costs of an already cheaper insurance policy are lowered even more by payments from your employer. Lastly, insurance premiums for workplace insurance policies are generally taken directly out of your paychecks. This means there is no worrying about paying the bill on time.

If you qualify for medical insurance at work, you should give very serious thought to signing up for one of these policies.

8.7 Health Savings Accounts

Health Savings Accounts are a special bank account type that was recently created by an Act of Congress. These accounts are very similar in structure to the IRAs discussed in previous chapters. You are permitted to put money into the accounts before taxes and you are limited in terms of how much money you can contribute each year. However, there is a special twist with Health Savings Accounts. With Health Savings Accounts, you are permitted to make withdrawals to pay for qualified medical expenses (i.e. cosmetic surgery does not apply). To do this, these accounts are often provided with a debit card similar to your checking account.

To qualify for a Health Savings Account, you must have a "high deductible" insurance policy. What this generally means is that you must have (and be able to prove) a medical insurance policy with a deductible over $1,000.

The idea behind this account type is an interesting one. While medical insurance can be expensive, having a high deductible policy will lower your monthly payments considerably. This is because you will not use your insurance for simple flu related medical visits. Instead you will pay for these out of your Health Savings Account. What your policy will do is protect you from the disaster of serious medical problems. In the event that you are hospitalized and large bills are generated, your insurance policy will kick in and cover the bills.

While this combination of insurance policy and bank account is not for everyone it is worth considering and does offer you another option for meeting your medical insurance needs. This can be a great way to lower your monthly insurance bills while protecting yourself from financial ruin. To find a policy with a deductible high enough to permit you to open a health savings account, talk to your insurance agent and to open a health savings account, talk to your bank.

8.8 Finding an Insurance Agent

Finding an insurance agent is simple. However, you need to be cautious and guarantee that your insurance agent is someone you trust who will recommend only policies that you need. To do this, seek the counsel of your friends and family. Their experiences can benefit you greatly.

If your friends and family can't provide you with any help, don't be afraid to use the phonebook. Meet with several agents and see what policies they recommend for you. Get a quote ***in writing***. Meet with several other agents and see what they recommend. Compare all of these quotes and see which agent can offer the best value.

Insurance agents need to be licensed before they can sell policies. States issue licenses through either their department of commerce or state. In addition each state maintains a database of each and every insurance agent licensed by that state. This can be an excellent resource when searching for an insurance agent. You can see if the agent you have chosen has any formal complaints lodged against them for poor business practices. If they do, avoid doing business with them.

Conclusion

If you are dedicated and save every dime you can and invest wisely over the next five years you may reach a point where you are financially independent. Then, disaster strikes. There is a fire in your apartment. All of your worldly possessions are destroyed. You do not have renter's insurance. How are you going to rebuild? You will be forced to use your savings and investments. You could very well find yourself back at zero. That is if you are financially independent to start with and have lots of savings.

If you do not have a lot of savings to begin with, you are in even more danger. Any unexpected problems such as fire, illness, or injury could put you seriously in debt in no time at all. You need to protect yourself and your family with insurance. Do not take this subject lightly.

Chapter 9
Taxes

Someone once said that there is nothing certain in life except for death and taxes. In America today, if you have an income, you will pay a portion of it to the government. Also, for most states you will pay a sales tax. You will also pay gas and property taxes if you drive a car or own a home. There are however, ways that you can lower your tax bill and delay paying it to your advantage. We are going to look at this subject in the following pages. Now, I must put in the standard warning. I am not a tax professional and the ideas presented in this chapter may not be appropriate to your situation. Before making serious decisions about your tax situation, consult a tax professional to obtain accurate, legal, and wise information that is relevant to your particular situation.

9.1 Types of Taxes

Federal Income Tax

The United States federal income tax is a percentage of your income that you pay to the federal government. This money is used to finance federal government activities such as defense, federal law enforcement, trade regulation, government office operations, etc. In 2007 the federal income tax rate fell between 10% and 35% of your income depending on the amount of money you earned. The U.S. federal income tax is based on a sliding scale. That means that the more money you make, the higher a percentage you pay in taxes.

Social Security Tax

There is another federal income tax that you pay specifically to the Social Security Administration. This is the United States social insurance program. This program was started during the Great Depression as a way of protecting the social status of America's citizens and preventing them from falling through the cracks. For example, if you are permanently disabled, you can receive payments from the Social Security Administration. Social Security also pays out retirement benefits. The idea is that you pay into the system during your working life and receive benefits once you retire. In 2007 this tax is 6.2% of wages but not to exceed $97,500.

Medicare Tax

The Medicare program is another federal program that is currently supported by a federal income tax. This program offers medical coverage to citizens that are over the age of 65 or who qualify in another manner. In 2007 this is a 2.9% tax. Half of the total tax or

1.45% is paid by the employee while the other 1.45% is paid by the employer.

State Income Tax

The state you live in may impose another tax on your income to support various state government activities. In 2007, 43 states had income tax programs of some kind. Some tax all of an individual's income while others tax only specific types of investment income.

State income taxes are calculated after federal income taxes have been taken out. For example, pretend you live in a state with a 5% income tax. Also pretend that you made $50,000 last year. If you paid $10,000 in federal taxes, you income that is subject to the state's 5% income tax would only be $40,000. This would result in a tax of $2,000 instead of $2,500.

Sales Tax

A sales tax is a very popular state tax method. This is a percentage above the purchase price of a good or service that is collected by the business to pass on to the government. Many states draw the majority of their operating income from taxes of this type. Currently, 44 states have a sales tax program whereby purchasers pay the tax amount. Hawaii has a slightly different program whereby the business pays the tax amount.

In 2007 the states that do not have a sales tax program are Oregon, Montana, Alaska, Delaware and New Hampshire.

Gasoline Tax

Gasoline is taxed in this country. Gas is taxed twice. One tax is by the federal government and one is by the state where you purchase the fuel. In 2005 the federal gas tax was raised to 18.4 cents per gallon. As of the writing of this book that is the current rate. The amount of tax imposed by states varies widely with an average of 22 cents per gallon.

Fuel taxes are an important source of government funding. The majority of money collected from these programs is used to pay for highway and bridge construction and maintenance.

Property Tax

If you own property you will also pay property taxes. These are taxes that are paid to fund local essential services such as police, fire, and emergency medical. Property taxes are also often used to support the education system in your county as well.

The tax rate for property taxes is set each year. The actual amount of tax that you will pay is calculated by taking the home's value (this is established each year by a county assessor) and multiplying it by the tax rate. One nice feature of many property tax programs is the ability to pay over several installments during the year. This can eliminate the burden of having to pay in one lump sum.

9.2 Tax Withholding

Some taxes, like sales tax, are paid immediately. Some taxes are paid throughout the year like property taxes. Federal and state income taxes are due on April 15th of each year. If April 15th is not a business day the tax due date is extended to the next weekday. For example if April 15th is a Saturday, the actual tax due date would be Monday April 17th. Never will it be shortened to April 14th.

Taxes due in one lump sum on one specific day can be a problem for a lot of folks. Many people have trouble planning ahead and setting aside the money that they will need to pay in taxes to state and federal governments. To alleviate this problem, there is a program in place called "tax withholding".

State and federal taxes are usually income taxes that are calculated based on your paychecks. To simplify the process and prevent you from coming up short when taxes are due, the IRS and state department of revenue take money directly out of your check each payday. This money is set aside in a special account called a "withholding account". This money is considered as tax money paid. When it is time to do your tax returns, you will pay additional money if enough has not been withheld, or you will receive a refund if too much has been withheld.

The amount of money that is withheld from your check is set by you when you are first hired at a job. You will be required to fill out a tax form W-4. This form can be found at the IRS website (http://www.irs.gov). There are two pages to this document; unfortunately, employers will rarely provide you with the second. On the second page you will find an important worksheet. This worksheet will help you declare how much money you wish to have withheld. You can, under certain specific qualifying circumstances, opt to have no money withheld. Discuss these concerns with a qualified tax preparer before making any decisions.

On the form W-4 you can also elect to have a specific dollar amount withheld as well, in addition to the normal withholding rate. This is useful if you believe that you have not had enough money withheld during the current tax year and you need to play "catch up".

Image 1. This is the front page of the 2007 form W-4. This form is returned to your employer for their use in withholding tax money. This form contains complete instructions on to fill it out. If you are uncertain consult a tax preparer before filling out this form.

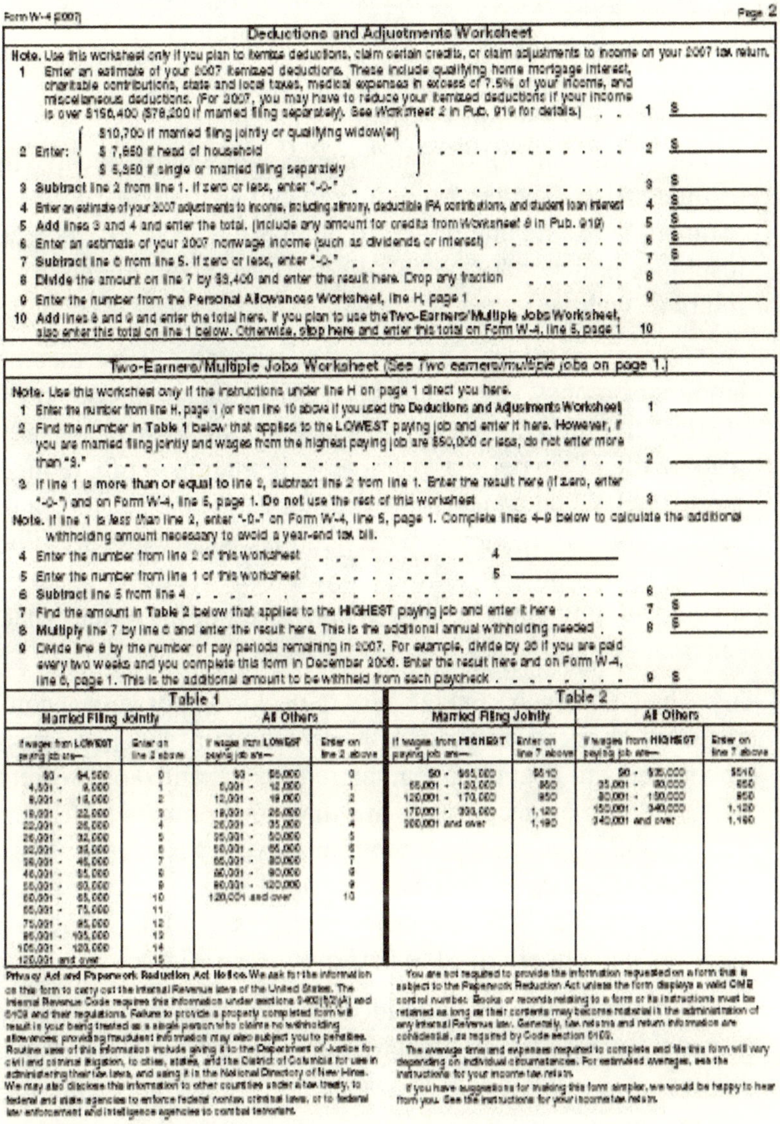
Form W-4 (2007) Page 2

Deductions and Adjustments Worksheet

Note. Use this worksheet only if you plan to itemize deductions, claim certain credits, or claim adjustments to income on your 2007 tax return.

1 Enter an estimate of your 2007 itemized deductions. These include qualifying home mortgage interest, charitable contributions, state and local taxes, medical expenses in excess of 7.5% of your income, and miscellaneous deductions. (For 2007, you may have to reduce your itemized deductions if your income is over $156,400 ($78,200 if married filing separately). See *Worksheet 2* in Pub. 919 for details.) . . . 1 $

2 Enter: { $10,700 if married filing jointly or qualifying widow(er); $ 7,850 if head of household; $ 5,350 if single or married filing separately } . . . 2 $

3 **Subtract** line 2 from line 1. If zero or less, enter "-0-" . . . 3 $

4 Enter an estimate of your 2007 adjustments to income, including alimony, deductible IRA contributions, and student loan interest 4 $

5 **Add** lines 3 and 4 and enter the total. (Include any amount for credits from *Worksheet 8* in Pub. 919) . 5 $

6 Enter an estimate of your 2007 nonwage income (such as dividends or interest) . . . 6 $

7 **Subtract** line 6 from line 5. If zero or less, enter "-0-" . . . 7 $

8 **Divide** the amount on line 7 by $3,400 and enter the result here. Drop any fraction . . . 8

9 Enter the number from the **Personal Allowances Worksheet**, line H, page 1 . . . 9

10 **Add** lines 8 and 9 and enter the total here. If you plan to use the **Two-Earners/Multiple Jobs Worksheet**, also enter this total on line 1 below. Otherwise, **stop here** and enter this total on Form W-4, line 5, page 1 10

Two-Earners/Multiple Jobs Worksheet (See *Two earners/multiple jobs* on page 1.)

Note. Use this worksheet *only* if the instructions under line H on page 1 direct you here.

1 Enter the number from line H, page 1 (or from line 10 above if you used the **Deductions and Adjustments Worksheet**) 1

2 Find the number in **Table 1** below that applies to the **LOWEST** paying job and enter it here. **However**, if you are married filing jointly and wages from the highest paying job are $50,000 or less, do not enter more than "3." . . . 2

3 If line 1 is **more than or equal to** line 2, subtract line 2 from line 1. Enter the result here (if zero, enter "-0-") and on Form W-4, line 5, page 1. **Do not** use the rest of this worksheet . . . 3

Note. If line 1 is *less than* line 2, enter "-0-" on Form W-4, line 5, page 1. Complete lines 4–9 below to calculate the additional withholding amount necessary to avoid a year-end tax bill.

4 Enter the number from line 2 of this worksheet . . . 4

5 Enter the number from line 1 of this worksheet . . . 5

6 **Subtract** line 5 from line 4 . . . 6

7 Find the amount in **Table 2** below that applies to the **HIGHEST** paying job and enter it here . . . 7 $

8 **Multiply** line 7 by line 6 and enter the result here. This is the additional annual withholding needed . . 8 $

9 Divide line 8 by the number of pay periods remaining in 2007. For example, divide by 26 if you are paid every two weeks and you complete this form in December 2006. Enter the result here and on Form W-4, line 6, page 1. This is the additional amount to be withheld from each paycheck . . . 9 $

Table 1

Married Filing Jointly: If wages from LOWEST paying job are—	Enter on line 2 above	All Others: If wages from LOWEST paying job are—	Enter on line 2 above
$0 - $4,500	0	$0 - $6,000	0
4,501 - 9,000	1	6,001 - 12,000	1
9,001 - 18,000	2	12,001 - 19,000	2
18,001 - 22,000	3	19,001 - 26,000	3
22,001 - 26,000	4	26,001 - 35,000	4
26,001 - 32,000	5	35,001 - 50,000	5
32,001 - 38,000	6	50,001 - 65,000	6
38,001 - 46,000	7	65,001 - 80,000	7
46,001 - 55,000	8	80,001 - 90,000	8
55,001 - 60,000	9	90,001 - 120,000	9
60,001 - 65,000	10	120,001 and over	10
65,001 - 75,000	11		
75,001 - 95,000	12		
95,001 - 105,000	13		
105,001 - 120,000	14		
120,001 and over	15		

Table 2

Married Filing Jointly: If wages from HIGHEST paying job are—	Enter on line 7 above	All Others: If wages from HIGHEST paying job are—	Enter on line 7 above
$0 - $65,000	$510	$0 - $35,000	$510
65,001 - 120,000	850	35,001 - 80,000	850
120,001 - 170,000	950	80,001 - 150,000	950
170,001 - 300,000	1,120	150,001 - 340,000	1,120
300,001 and over	1,190	340,001 and over	1,190

Privacy Act and Paperwork Reduction Act Notice. We ask for the information on this form to carry out the Internal Revenue laws of the United States. The Internal Revenue Code requires this information under sections 3402(f)(2)(A) and 6109 and their regulations. Failure to provide a properly completed form will result in your being treated as a single person who claims no withholding allowances; providing fraudulent information may also subject you to penalties. Routine uses of this information include giving it to the Department of Justice for civil and criminal litigation, to cities, states, and the District of Columbia for use in administering their tax laws, and using it in the National Directory of New Hires. We may also disclose this information to other countries under a tax treaty, to federal and state agencies to enforce federal nontax criminal laws, or to federal law enforcement and intelligence agencies to combat terrorism.

You are not required to provide the information requested on a form that is subject to the Paperwork Reduction Act unless the form displays a valid OMB control number. Books or records relating to a form or its instructions must be retained as long as their contents may become material in the administration of any Internal Revenue law. Generally, tax returns and return information are confidential, as required by Code section 6103.

The average time and expenses required to complete and file this form will vary depending on individual circumstances. For estimated averages, see the instructions for your income tax return.

If you have suggestions for making this form simpler, we would be happy to hear from you. See the instructions for your income tax return.

Image 2. This is the second page of the 2007 Form W-4. This page contains a worksheet that is very useful in determining how much tax money you should have withheld.

9.3 Declaring All Your Income

It is essential that you declare all of your taxable income. There are several reasons that you want to do this.

Firstly, if you are injured on the job your disability benefits will be based on your previous year's tax documents. If you are not honest and do not declare all of your income, you will not receive the amount of financial assistance that you need and are entitled to. In a similar manner, if you are attempting to purchase a disability income insurance policy, your potential benefits are determined by your tax return as well.

Another consideration when declaring all of your income is the amount of money you can borrow. Now, I have already been quite clear on my thoughts on debt, however, there may be a need to borrow in your life. One perfect example is the purchase of a home with a mortgage. When considering your loan application, the bank will look at the amount of money you declared last year when deciding how much money you can borrow. If you have not declared all of your income, you may not be able to borrow all of the money that you are seeking.

The last reason to make sure to declare all of your income is the IRS may check up on you. The IRS maintains an enormous staff off accountants to guarantee that tax returns are filled out correctly and truthfully. They accomplish this through a process called an "audit". An audit is a thorough investigation of your tax return. This can be an unpleasant process if you have not been honest on your taxes. You can be subject to large monetary penalties in addition to the extra tax money that you will need to pay.

It may seem like a good idea to lower your tax bill by hiding some of your income, but, in the long run it can be a costly mistake. Don't make it.

9.4 Tax Deductions

There are legal means to lower your tax bill. These methods are called "deductions". A deduction is used to lower your taxable income. Let's look at an example. Imagine that you earned $50,000 this year. At 15% you will pay $7,500 in taxes. You have donated $5,000 to a qualified charitable organization, which is a tax deduction. This entitles you to lower your taxable income by the amount of money you donated. So, as a result of your donation and the deduction your taxable income will only be $45,000 or a total tax bill of $6,750.

Now, you are probably wondering why this is allowed. In a nutshell the federal government encourages certain behaviors with deductions. The deductions effectively lower the costs of certain activities and makes them more attractive. Tax deductions are commonly used to encourage citizens to:

- Go to school
- Start a business
- Donate to charity
- Save money for retirement

There are many, many, potential deductions that you can take advantage of. The 2007 federal tax code is a long, complicated document and a professional tax preparer can help you identify all the deductions that you qualify for. We will however, explore a few potential deductions that are of particular interest.

Education

If you are reading this book it is a distinct possibility that you are, have been, or wish to be a student. Continuing your education can be a great way to increase your earning potential but it is not free. In fact, it can be expensive, even discouragingly so. To help you go back to school, increase you earning potential, and just maybe invent a new artificial heart, the government offers tax deductions for education. You will receive documentation in January of the current year for the previous tax year, from your school. Take this with you when you have your taxes prepared.

Save Money on Taxes By Saving Money

I am not the only one that wants you to save money. The federal government wants you to save money too. Specifically, the government wants you to save money for retirement. Saving money for retirement now will help prevent you from becoming a burden to society when you are older. Also, the money that you save can be loaned out by banks. This means more factories can be built, businesses started and jobs created. So this is really a benefit to everyone, starting with you.

Now you cannot go and save money any way you want and take a tax deduction. You must save your money in special accounts. These accounts are the Individual Retirement Account (IRA) and the 401(k). Placing money into either of these account types will give you a tax deduction in the amount of the money that you deposit.

Now there are limits, in 2008, you can place a maximum of $5,000 in an IRA and $15,500 into a 401(k). By act of Congress, the maximum amount that you can legally contribute to your IRA will increase by $500 per year afterwards. If you happen to be married, these numbers and the amount you can deduct may be subject to change so, again, contact your tax planner before making any decisions or taking any action. Undoing a mistake in this regard can be very expensive. There is an immediate 10% penalty for withdrawals prior to the age of 59.5 (yes that is correct), in addition to any taxes you will need to pay.

There is also a catch. While you put the money into these account types tax free, you will have to pay taxes on the money that you remove from the account. You will also have to remove mandatory minimum amounts when you turn 70 years of age. However, for the current benefit of a tax deduction, plus additional money to invest for retirement, these are small trade offs.

9.5 Professional Tax Preparation

Professional tax preparation is a must if you are planning to take advantage of tax deductions. This process is often called "itemizing". This service will cost you a bit of money, generally on a per form basis, but it is well worth it.

The first thing you buy when you take advantage of a professional tax preparer is peace of mind. The federal tax code is complicated and it is very easy for an untrained individual to make a costly mistake. Hiring a professional significantly lowers the possibility that mistakes will happen.

In addition to lowering the chances of mistakes, a professional can also help you in the event of an audit. This advocate on your side to offer advice ad counsel during a difficult time such as an audit can be very helpful and well worth a small fee.

Finding a tax preparer is very similar to finding an insurance agent. The easiest and often best place to find one is your friends and family. Everyone who has a job pays taxes, so it is a good chance one of these people knows someone they would be happy to recommend. Also, like insurance agents, tax preparers have to be licensed. You can check out the credentials of your preparer with either your state government or your state's tax preparer association.

Conclusion

Taxes are a fact of life that you will need to deal with. Planning ahead will help you to minimize the amount of money that you will pay to the government. The strategies discussed in this chapter are only the tip of the iceberg. Every year the tax laws are added to and changed. This provides additional opportunities to save money on taxes for the following year.

For now, since you are most likely a tax payer, focus on finding a professional tax preparer that you like and trust. This will lay the groundwork for sound tax planning by providing you with a source of competent, informed and trustworthy advice.

Afterword

This book was about getting your financial affairs in order. The lessons contained in it were learned by me as I went along. I made mistakes and you will profit from them. If you work hard I am confident that you can get your affairs in order and overcome your financial problems. While you are digging out of debt and beginning to save money, consider making some long term goals to improve your situation. Very briefly, four ideas are presented below.

Once you have dug yourself out of debt and saved a little money, you can begin to give serious thought to repairing your credit. Now, you are probably wondering just why you care about your credit anyway. I did, after all write a good deal about not using credit and relying on your own financial resources. Well, the truth of the matter is that credit is an extremely important part of life in America today and having good credit can be a great asset.

For example, consider buying a house. After reading this book, you may become an expert saver. It could happen. However, it may take you 25 years or more to save enough money to buy a home. What this means is that you will have to borrow some money to buy a home before that point. To do this, you will need to have good credit.

Consider also, starting a business. You may be debt free with some money in the bank and a great idea for a business. However, with poor credit you will not be able to obtain start-up money.

Bad credit can hamper you in quite a few ways. Most banks will check your credit history before opening a bank account (even a safe deposit box) for you. So, it would be nice to have good credit for lots of reasons.

You may feel that you can do nothing, but you would be dead wrong. There are many good books out there about credit repair that you can do yourself. Since beginning to write this book I have used a number of these. Your results may vary, but mine have been very good.

You may also want to give some very strong thought to going back to school. No matter what your level of education thus far in life, you can benefit from more. Perhaps you would like to go and get your GED. Receiving technical training in some form or another can free you from low paying dead end jobs. A Bachelor's degree can open many doors that had been previously closed and a Master's degree will almost certainly mean an increase in pay.

All of these ideas may have crossed your mind but you have no idea of where to start. If you need to finish high school, get a two year degree or receive technical training, there is no better place to start than you local community college. These institutions offer very good education and can be a stepping stone to finishing a four year degree. These colleges offer very professional and knowledgeable advisors who will counsel you on all the aspects of returning to school. They can present information on:

- Academic Programs
- Financial Aid
- Grants
- Class Schedules

The information that they provide can be of enormous value and you would be wise to listen to their advice.

If you are planning to complete a four year degree or master's degree, you will need to seek this same type of advice at a local university. Make sure that you ask about financing your return to academia. In addition, see if any of these classes are offered in an Internet or distance learning format. This is becoming increasingly popular with upper division classes and can save you a bit of time and driving.

Consider working towards buying a home. Owning your own home has many advantages over renting. For example, each month you won more of your home and can borrow money against it if the need should arise. In addition, it is not uncommon for homes to increase in value. This means that if you own your home for five years and decide to sell it, there is a good chance you will be selling it at a profit. These profits can easily run into the tens of thousands of dollars. Have you ever heard of someone renting an apartment that can boast of that?

To actually buy a home, you will need to have relatively good credit. Work hard at getting your record cleaned up first. Next, you will most likely need a down payment. You can buy a home with 100% borrowed money, but it is harder. Traditionally, down payments are 10%-20% of the purchase price of the home. You should plan on having this much money to use as a down payment. Additionally, you should plan on having at least $10,000 more to ensure that you have a financial cushion, once you have bought the home.

Lastly, give some thought to starting a business of some kind. This book is not about how to do that and you will need to do lots of research and planning. Take some business classes at a community college if your previous education has not covered it. Starting and running a business can be very rewarding. Firstly, it can be very profitable if done properly. Secondly, owning a business can provide you with independence and security. Many millionaires in this country did not start that way. Instead, they started businesses and worked hard at them.

I feel that I have provided you with many tools to improve your financial situation. It may be rough and take some adjustments but I am confident that you can do it. As a final note, I love to hear from my readers. If you feel that there are other subjects that need to be covered, perhaps in later editions, please drop me a line via the publisher of this book. Also, every effort has been made to ensure that this work is free from error. However, if any errors should be found please let me know as well. Thanks for reading.

-Peter Wilmore